In that Moment...
FINISH IT!
Biblical Tools for Christian Women When Faced with Life's Decisions

In that Moment...
FINISH IT!
Biblical Tools for Christian Women When Faced with Life's Decisions

Juanita E. Davis

Davis Bookshelf
Galesburg, Illinois

In That Moment... FINISH IT!
Copyright © 2023-2025 by Juanita E. Davis
First Edition: September 2023

All rights reserved. No part of this book may be reproduced or transmitted in any form or by any means without written permission of the publisher, except in brief quotes or reviews. Unless otherwise noted, all Scripture is taken from the New King James Version of the Bible® (NKJV). Copyright © 1982 by Thomas Nelson. Used by permission.

Published by Davis Bookshelf
401 E. Main St., Ste. 163, Galesburg IL 61401 www.juanitaedavis.com
Tel. (309) 509-8881
E-mail: Info.davisbookshelf@gmail.com
Facebook: Davis Bookshelf LLC and Juanita E. Davis

Book cover design: Phil Coles Independent Design

ISBN: 9798218368012 (Hardcover)

Library of Congress Control Number: 2024903271

Published in the United States of America.

Dedication

This book is dedicated to Sara.

Acknowledgments

First and above all else, I would like to acknowledge my Lord and Savior, Jesus Christ. Without Him, without His Spirit guiding me, and without His power at work in and His fruit at work through me, I would have made many more in-the-moment rash and unwise decisions than I have to date. I thank God that for all the commands that He, the Father in Heaven, has given His children that He has not left us inept to do them, but has given us help in the Holy Spirit. Jesus is my everything.

To my husband Randy, the man of my prayers. I would like to thank you for believing in me and for, at times, believing in what God has said to me more than I did. In moments when I was tempted to make rash, emotional decisions and quit, at the risk of changing the trajectory of not only mine but others' lives, you encouraged me to stand and finish it (whatever *it* was at the time). I thank God for you, man of God, and for the Christlike character trait of steadfastness you possess. In Christ, you stood and encouraged me to stand, even in moments when you, too, may have been tempted to give up and quit. I love you much!

To Dorice Houston. Thank you for believing in every vision that God gave to Pastor Randy and me from the big vision of *Dominion House Ministries*, my first book, the Unoffended Crusades, and now this book. We love you, and we thank God for you. You stood with us, prayed with and for us, believed in us – *a remnant* – and you continue to do so. To God be the glory!

To Vanita O'Neal and Christy Davis Knox. Thank each of you for pushing me with one question, *"Have you written anything else?"*

To Juanetta Jackson, Juanita Whaley, Rev. Dr. Karen Tinsley, and Dana Johnson. Thank you all for not counting it robbery of your time to read the manuscript, days before the 2023 release!

To Carla Kincaid and the *Reconciled Women's Ministry* of Neuse Baptist Church, Kinston, North Carolina. Thank you for your invaluable feedback after reading the book as a group!

To LaDeidre Jenkins, Pamela McQueen, Jeanette Jackson, and Destiny Thomas. Thank you for praying with and for me from the time I shared the idea of this book with you to its publication.

To the ladies of *Gracious Gatherings Book Club*, thank you all for nine glorious weeks of reading each chapter with me and ***finishing it***!

Lastly, to *Hunter Entertainment Network (Publishing)*. Thank you for taking on the task of the initial publication of this book!

Love and blessings to you all!

Endorsements

To God be the Glory. This book, "**IN THAT MOMENT… FINISH IT!**" is amazing from cover to cover… from the introduction to the final prayer, you will find encouragement, wisdom, and revelation. What should you do or say right now, in this very moment? The author skillfully depicts the lives of nine fictional characters who are asked that very question and through the author's unique format, you get to determine the "perfect" answer for them using the carefully chosen scriptures at the end of each chapter. As you find yourself, or others that you know, revealed in these chapters, this book reminds us that we actually live in that moment… *finish it* with choices that give God the glory!!!

Rev. Dr. Karen L. Tinsley, Pastor
Anointed Vision Christian Church
Goldsboro, NC

In That Moment... FINISH IT: Biblical Tools for Christian Women When Faced With Life's Decisions, by Juanita E. Davis, is a practical guide for navigating contemporary challenges. Juanita Davis has given us nine chapters of real-life stories which engage the reader and ask us to think biblically about the outcome. The unique format, with the stories left unfinished, allows the reader the time and space to reflect on their own possible responses to each situation. From the temptations of the single woman, to questions of marriage, divorce, abuse, not to mention the difficult issues surrounding church life (and many more), Juanita Davis has indeed given us a valuable tool for responding and acting biblically in a confused and confusing world.

Dana M. Johnson
Manager, *Brighter Life Bookshoppe*
Galesburg, IL

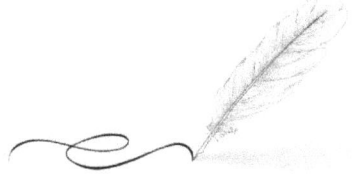

In That Moment… Finish It! is a great reminder that knowing what we need to do in our heads and doing what we need to do in our hearts can be miles apart. That distance between our heads and our hearts can be conflicting thoughts that are a mix of righteous and unrighteous outcomes. Each chapter is asking, "What say you? What will you choose?" It is in making those seemingly unimportant decisions that can change the entire course of our lives. **In that Moment… Finish It!** reminds us to pay attention to the details. It forces us to think through how we are going to choose, in those small moments, to propel us further in or out of sin. Additionally, the biblical teachings explain the depth of God's love for us demonstrated in His Word by showing concern in all of our decisions, every moment of our lives, down to the smallest details!

Vanita O'Neal, MA, MSW
Social Worker
Los Angeles, CA

Foreword

In John chapter 15, verses 4 and 7, Jesus commands believers to "Abide in Him…" This is how we are expected to successfully get through this life. Looking from birth to our last day and trying to live like Christ over that time can seem daunting. Fortunately for us, God gives us a manageable unit of time to navigate through, so it will be less intimidating. All we need to do is manage the day before us. Matthew 6:34 is our reminder to not get caught up in tomorrow's issues. So, that leaves us with today and how we get through today. There is a good reason why we pray, "…give us this day our daily bread…" We get through our days by living *moment by moment*.

<u>In That Moment… Finish It!</u> is the perfect example of how we apply God's Word to our lives. The issues and situations in our lives come at us in the "right now". When we remember to abide in Christ as His Word abides in us, we can and will stand ready to seek God's outcome when those moments arise.

The challenge of the accounts in this book is to *finish it* according to the Word of God. The purpose of challenging the reader is not to see if there is a right or wrong answer, but to search the Scriptures and present a righteous response to the situation. We cannot practice for, or hope to be prepared for, every possible scenario that might arise; but, when we abide in Christ and His Word abides in us, *in that moment…* we will *finish it*, and God will be glorified.

God has blessed Juanita with the idea for the uniquely original format of this book. It is our prayer that in reading it and searching the Scriptures that the reader will be inspired to dive deeper into the Word of God, seeking the life-changing truths it contains. We also desire that the reader will grow in the depth of knowledge and understanding of who God is. Finally, we hope that the disciple of Christ will be equipped, encouraged, and empowered to become a disciple-maker.

Pastor Randy H. Davis,
Blessed husband of Juanita E. Davis

Table of Contents

Introduction 1
Chapter 1: Out of the Fire 5
Chapter 2: Signs 17
Chapter 3: Holy Matrimony 29
Chapter 4: For Better or For Worse? 39
Chapter 5: To Give or Not to Give 49
Chapter 6: Birthing Greatness 63
Chapter 7: By Faith 73
Chapter 8: Creator of All, Father to Some 85
Chapter 9: Just as Much Now as Then 97
Meet the Author
Prayer

Introduction

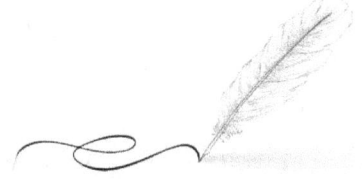

Have you ever heard about a bad decision that someone made, and said, "If I was her, I would've..."? Well, guess what! You will never be *her*, you can never actually think for *her,* but you can advise *her*. However, first, you would need to think like Christ. An often overlooked truth about our Lord is that He had a soul. Thus, He had emotions. When Jesus came to the earth as God incarnate, by way of Mary's womb, He put on something that was totally new to Him. A flesh suit, or a body; and that flesh suit came with everything that it comes with for you and me—soul, emotions, mind, and will. Yet, Jesus is our example for how we can successfully subdue the flesh, bring it into subjection to the Holy Spirit, and finish our *in that moment*'s according to God's will and plan. In That Moment...FINISH IT! is a finished book containing the unfinished stories of nine fictional women. Though fictional, these nine women face real-life issues–issues that none of us are immune to. None of the nine dilemmas may ever darken the doorsteps of your life personally, but what about your sister, your mother, your friend, the neighbor, or the stranger that you might meet? What is gleaned from this book might not be applicable to you, but it could be the answer that someone close to you might need… *in that moment.*

When I began writing this book, I had no blueprint. The Holy Spirit said, "Write," and I wrote. As I was writing Chapter One and got close to what I thought was the end of it, I realized I had no ending for it. God had not given me one. So, I decided to move on to Chapter Two until He did. However, as with the first chapter, I got close to what I thought was the end of it, and had no ending for it either! That's when it dawned on me. I was not supposed to finish the chapters. You are! Each chapter is a tool for training us to harness our emotions and be Spirit-led when facing **and** making life's decisions. That is why at the end of each chapter there is a list containing a mix of Bible verses that were either referenced in the chapter or that can be used to finish each story, biblically. There is also a journaling section for note-taking or writing the finish that you come up with. The concept of this book is mind-blowing! I compare it to the times I gave birth to my sons. With each delivery, I looked at them and thought, "Did something so beautiful and miraculous come out of *me*?"

That's how I see this book. God conceived it in me and has birthed it through me—and it's marvelous! I pray that you will enjoy finishing the stories on your own, with a friend, a book club, or your women's Bible study group. More than that, I pray that you would be equipped and empowered to FINISH IT! God's way.

Love you to Life,

Juanita

*"Blessed is the man who walks not in the counsel of the ungodly,
Nor stands in the way of sinners,
Nor sits in the seat of the scornful;
But his delight is in the law of the LORD,
And in His law he meditates day and night.
He shall be like a tree planted by the rivers of water,
that brings forth its fruit in its season,
whose leaf also shall not wither;
And whatever he does shall prosper."* – Psalm 1:1-3

Chapter 1

Out of the Fire

As Anna Lisa got into her car that Sunday morning, she was immediately overcome not only by guilt, which was usual, but also something else. She had a deep longing to hear the preached Word of God. Being overcome by guilt was a usual occurrence for Anna Lisa because guilt was an all too familiar companion of hers. This Sunday morning was no different from most other Sunday mornings, or any other random morning, when she found herself leaving her boyfriend's house. "Or is he my boyfriend," she thought to herself.

Thomas was a guy that Anna Lisa had known for about a year. They met on New Year's Eve, at a club, and they hit it off, at least physically, right away. Theirs was not a typical boyfriend-girlfriend kind of relationship though, and that is why Anna Lisa was not sure what label to put on Thomas. Was he her boyfriend, or was he just someone to kick it with? She wanted more with him and although she was seeing him exclusively, she was not so sure that he was seeing her exclusively. That bothered Anna Lisa, but she accepted what was because she was lonely; and against all her moral and sensible convictions, she continued to answer Thomas' late-night and random calls to have her loneliness pacified.

Anna Lisa was well-educated, with a Doctorate from a very prestigious university. She graduated top of her class from high school, from university, and from her doctorate program, and she was a very successful and sought-after entrepreneurial consultant. At the age of twenty-eight, she was able to buy her first house, and she owned a couple of luxury vehicles. She, along with her two younger brothers and sister, took great care of their mother, a widow since Anna Lisa's senior year of high school. Anna Lisa's father was a good man to his wife and children. He had worked hard, and he loved the Lord. He had also set a godly standard for Anna Lisa and her sister of how a man should treat a woman. He did so not only by how he treated their mother but also by how he treated his daughters. The only problem with that was that it seemed as though when her father died, good men like him became extinct.

Anna Lisa's father loved the Lord, and he let nothing get in the way of that relationship. He had also been a man of his word. If he said it, it was as good as done as soon as the words left his mouth. A Bible verse that he stood on was Psalm 15:1-4, which says that *'those who may worship in the Lord's sanctuary and enter His presence on His holy hill keep their promises even when it hurts.'* Unlike her father, Thomas was not a man of his word, but a man of many words. He had whispered many sweet nothings into Anna Lisa's ear. They were just that though– nothing–because nothing ever came of them.

Out of the Fire

One way that he did compare to her father was that he was a hard worker. Thomas owned his own architectural firm and was very sought after not only for his skill, but for his knowledge, as well. At forty-four, he was almost exactly ten years older than Anna Lisa. He had no children and had never been married, two things that he often told Anna Lisa were desires but not priorities for him. However, he also told her that if they ever became priorities, he would want to marry her and have a family with her. That *if* was no guarantee; but again, Anna Lisa was lonely and that *if* was good enough for her. Or was it?

Thomas was not a bad person. He was just lost and confused, "The same as me," Anna Lisa reasoned. He, like her, had grown up going to church; and, according to him, he once had a strong, close relationship with the Lord. In fact, he knew that he was called to be a pastor and teacher, and that had been his dream as a young boy. However, once he graduated from college and became successful in his career, he stopped attending church services and Bible studies. His personal relationship with God began to dwindle as well, at least his side of it anyway. One day, he just stopped talking to God altogether, except for when it seemed like a deal was going to fall through. Just like with Anna Lisa, Thomas' career, success, and money had become his gods.

As Anna Lisa began the short drive home, the longing to hear the preached Word of God became so much stronger. It was a longing so deep that she knew that tuning in to an online or televised sermon would not suffice. So, after arriving home and taking that all too familiar walk of shame before her younger sister who lived with her, she took a shower and got dressed. She knew exactly what church she was going to attend, too! Not wanting to be late, she grabbed a set of her car keys, and raced out the door. She was desperate to have that deep longing within fulfilled. Neither Thomas nor his meaningless words could fill it, and that is why she left him most every Sunday morning (and any occasional other morning) for the past year, feeling emptier than when she had gone.

The church's parking lot was not very full at all. Anna Lisa could count on both hands how many cars were there, and she wondered if she might have missed the service. However, just as she was about to put her car in drive and drive away, another car pulled into the parking lot and parked right beside her on the passenger side. "Now, out of all the empty spaces in this parking lot, they would choose to park right beside me! And close, too," Anna Lisa complained out loud to herself. She was just about to drive away when she heard a tap on her passenger side window. She looked up to see an older woman with a very familiar face standing there. It was Mrs. Parker, one of her business mentors. Mrs. Parker had invited Anna Lisa to her church several times during their mentorship, but Anna Lisa never went. Embarrassed because it had taken so long for her to accept the invitation, Anna Lisa let down her window. Not wanting to explain why she had waited so long to come, she wondered if she could have just gotten what she was longing for at home on the T.V., or the internet.

"Hey, Sweetie! It's SO good to see you," Mrs. Parker exclaimed. "You're early, but come on in. That way, you can get a good seat because in about thirty minutes, it's going to start to fill up fast with folks wanting to hear the Word." If it bothered her that Anna Lisa had taken so long to accept her invitation, Mrs. Parker certainly did not let on. Because of it, Anna Lisa was able to relax and not feel so ashamed anymore.

Out of the Fire

Once inside the building, and against Mrs. Parker's insistence, Anna Lisa took a seat on the very last row of pews. It had been several years since she had been inside a church building, and as she sat and waited for the service to begin, she entertained church memories from her own childhood. She chuckled to herself as she thought about her and her siblings sitting on the front row with their mother. Their father was a deacon, so he usually sat off to the side of the sanctuary. He never sat so far away that he could not handle business with a misbehaving child or two though, and he did so with his eyes. There were many Sundays that at least one of his children would get the *you-just-wait-til-we-get-home* look from their father. That look would sober up not just her father's misbehaving child(ren), but any other misbehaving child in the congregation that happened to see it.

Sometimes, it would take her and her siblings a while to sober up though, especially those times that they would become riddled with what they called the "church giggles". Those were those giggles where you just could not stop giggling even if you wanted to, and they were usually the result of an outburst from one of the older members (including their parents) getting their shout on or yelling, "Amen," as the pastor preached. Why it was so funny to them, Anna Lisa could never figure out. Their parents always called it the folly of youth though and told them that one day, Jesus was gonna get such a hold of them, and them Him; that they would be the ones being laughed at for their outbursts. Getting back to reality, Anna Lisa noticed that more people had come into the church. She also realized that she had been so busy reminiscing that she did not notice when Mrs. Parker sat down beside her. She was sitting very close to her, almost too close for comfort... like how she had parked her car next to hers. However, Anna Lisa welcomed her closeness this time. There was something comforting and almost filling about it.

As the service began, the choir sung several songs, the ministers and deacons prayed and exhorted the people who were gathered, and then the pastor stood up to preach the sermon. By that time, Anna Lisa was not feeling as empty anymore. As the pastor began to speak, he looked very intently out over the congregation, and Anna Lisa felt that at one point, he was only looking at her. That's exactly why she sat all the way in the back… to hide. "Good morning to you all! We've been walking through the Bible, book by book, and today we are in the Book of Jude. This morning, the Holy Spirit reminded me of Nehemiah 8, and how the people took the Book of the Law to the priests and asked them to read it to them. He also told me that there was going to be one person here this morning who was longing for the preached Word; somebody who was feeling empty and knew that it wasn't their accomplishments, money, success, things, sex, or even other people that could fill them. They knew that only the preached Word of God, the Living Word of God, could do it. So, whoever you are, just know that God loves you enough to have us take that quick run all the way back from the Book of Jude to Nehemiah to spur just one soul–**you**–on to the finish line. That void that you were feeling can only be filled by God, and you have done well to follow your soul's longing for Him."

"For the sake of a sermon title, we will call this, *Out of the Fire*. So, if you will turn with me to the Book of Jude, I'm going to read it in its entirety." The preacher then chuckled, "Don't worry. It's only a chapter-long."

Out of the Fire

He read the chapter, or rather Book, and then expounded on verses twenty-two and twenty-three, which read,

"And on some have compassion, making a distinction; but others save with fear, pulling them out of the fire, hating even the garment defiled by the flesh."

Then, looking intently over the congregation, the pastor said, "Going back to Nehemiah 8:1-12, I want to ask a question, especially to the one who came so desperately wanting to hear the preached Word. Can you see yourself in verse one? You see, just as all the people came together as one and told Ezra to bring out the Book of the Law of Moses, that is also what you did. Now, going back to the Book of Jude, do you understand that you are not here on your own volition? No, this is the Lord attempting, through me, to snatch you from the fire." The pastor continued, "You see, when Adam and Eve fell in the Garden of Eden, when God banished them, a void was made in their souls. They were no longer in the presence of God like they had been used to from their creation. We could say that it is comparable to when a loved one like a parent, a child, or someone else that's close to us dies. But the comparison stops there, because even though we can no longer be in that loved one's presence, even alive, they could not fill that void. The void that was made when Adam and Eve were banished was not just their void. It became a void for all mankind that came after them, including you and me. Only God can fill that void. Do you understand?"

At that point, Anna Lisa was convinced that the pastor was looking at and talking only to her. She realized that there was no hiding, not on a back pew of a crowded church, nor behind the fig leaves of success, degrees, money, things, and a continuum of one-nighters and some-timers with Thomas.

"Each of you are here because you know that there is more. I'm talking to every soul here, but especially to the ones in the fire right now. *"Deep calls unto deep at the noise of Your waterfalls."* That's Psalm 42:7. This morning, you woke up and you realized that the cry was much louder than it's ever been and that the longing was much deeper than you have ever experienced. Has the connection been made? Are you full yet?" The pastor ended the sermon by reading through the first twelve verses in Nehemiah 8, again. He read it with such passion, and all around her Anna Lisa could hear people crying. "It's just like in the Scriptures," she thought. It did not take her long to realize that she was in the number of mourners, as well.

Mrs. Parker was holding not only her hand now. She was holding Anna Lisa, and she whispered to her, "God did this just for you. He loves you." Anna Lisa sobbed uncontrollably as she thought of how she had sinned and stayed away from God for so long, how she had hurt Him. She thought back to those nights and times with Thomas and wondered why she had never answered God's call as readily as she had answered Thomas' calls.

As she began to sober up, the pastor's wife was before the congregation and speaking, "You've come today and reconnected with God. Now, will you stay connected to Him? Just as much as He's saying, 'Neither be ye sorry,' because He's that merciful, remember that He's also just." In James 4, it says that *"the Spirit who dwells in us yearns jealously and that God resists the proud, but He gives grace to the humble. Therefore, submit to God. Resist the devil and he will flee from you. Draw near to God and He will draw near to you. Cleanse your hands, you sinners; and purify your hearts, you double-minded. Lament and mourn and weep! Let your laughter be turned to mourning and your joy to gloom."* In other words, God is saying that if you resist Him and remain in your sin that you have reason enough to keep mourning. The passage ends with this: *"Humble yourselves in the sight of the Lord, and He will lift you up."* Will you be lifted up and out of the fire? After you leave here, will you remain lifted out, or will you return to the fire?"

At the pastor's wife's invitation, Anna Lisa went forward and recommitted her life to the Lord. Mrs. Parker walked with her, and afterward, they promised to keep in touch with one another. Although Anna Lisa got too busy with work the following week, Mrs. Parker called her twice. One of her phone calls came as Anna Lisa was on the phone with Thomas. He had called to say that he might have to see her on Friday instead of their usual Saturday night. After hanging up with him, she listened to Mrs. Parker's voicemail. She was calling to invite her to a women's fellowship on Friday night.

Late Friday afternoon, Anna Lisa's phone rang. It was Thomas. Earlier in the week, feeling emboldened and not caring whether she saw him or not, she had called Mrs. Parker back and told her that she would attend the women's fellowship with her. Now, as her phone rang, she held it and stared at it rather than answering it. "There will be other women's fellowships," she reasoned to herself. "Mrs. Parker will understand. This is going to be my only chance to see Thomas, and we don't have to… we don't have to… I mean, we can just have dinner and watch a movie. I'm strong enough to say, "No." Louder than her own reasoning and the lies, she heard a still small voice that sounded a lot like the pastor's wife quietly asking, "Will you remain lifted out, or will you return to the fire?"

In that moment, Anna Lisa answered her phone. "Hello, Thomas…"

FINISH IT!

Juanita E. Davis

READ

Bible verses that were referenced in the chapter:

- Nehemiah 8:1-12
- Psalm 42:7
- Psalm 15:1-4
- Matthew 5:6
- James 4:10
- Jude 1:20-24

Bible verses to consider when finishing this story:

- Psalm 1:1-3
- Proverbs 26:11
- 1 Corinthians 10:12-13
- 2 Timothy 2:22
- James 1:12-16
- 2 Peter 2:21-22

FINISH IT!

Chapter 2

Signs

Lena was convinced that Jason was the answer to the prayers that she had prayed to God, asking Him for her husband. She and Jason had not known one another for very long; but she just knew that he was the one, and he believed the same regarding her. As only God can do, Jason exceeded all her desired attributes for her husband to possess. He was very kind and respectful towards her. He was also patient, and she needed that, especially with the baggage that she was still in the process of unpacking from her life. He was not perfect. Some of his flaws were quite evident, but they were not turn offs or deal breakers. In fact, she was thankful to the Lord for each of them, because they reminded her that Jason was not her god and could never be. His flaws helped her to keep him in the right perspective.

Lena had experienced a tough childhood and an even tougher past five years, which meant that she had her share of issues to work through. She had been raped as a young girl by a trusted family friend and leader in their church, and that led to promiscuity in her teens to her early twenties. During those years, she was forever looking for love but never finding it. Truth be told, she would not have recognized love if she had found it, because she did not know what it looked like. As she was finding what felt like love, and that in all the wrong places and guys, she was as content as she could be though, at least emotionally. Or so she thought. Lena went into relationships giving her all... well, mostly. Although she had only been in three serious relationships and had been faithful, totally committed, and everything but a wife in those three, there had been flings with other men in between those relationships. In giving her all at the start of the relationships, the one thing that Lena withdrew quicker than her presence was her trust when there was even a hint of any of her past boyfriends being unfaithful to her.

It is backwards how the devil will use the same person that is supposed to show and teach a young girl what love and trust look like to be the same one who distorts her view of the two. After she gave her life to the Lord at the age of twenty-four, Lena realized that being raped had primed her to be nothing more than a prostitute. She prostituted her body, with the payment being emotional acceptance and companionship. It had very little to do with sex. What Lena had learned in that one horrible and traumatic moment of her life was that love was not something to be experienced but felt, sexually. In attending church services regularly now (to include weekly Bible Study) and in spending quality time with God through reading His Word and prayer for insight, Lena realized that what she had gleaned from that experience was a distorted view of love. More than it is something to be felt physically, love is to be experienced spiritually and relationally. She learned that as humans and emotional beings that our feelers can be wrong, a lot of the

Signs

time! Experiencing love was in truth supposed to be about experiencing God, and most often through others, because He is love.

Can love, can God, be felt? Most assuredly! However, God desires to be seen and experienced spiritually and relationally, and she learned from her pastor and in a personal study of the Word that this is why Jesus said, "Blessed are the pure in heart, for they shall see God." God desires that we see Him and that we know Him. Lena knew that all too well. When going through a recent crisis, she did not always feel that God was with her or that He was even hearing her prayers. The situation was so big that it obstructed her view at times, but it was when she took her eyes off the situation and lifted them up and away that she saw God. She saw that the "hills" that she lifted her eyes to were not her help, but that God beyond them was and is. The hills only gave her reason to look up and away from the situation. Doing that allowed her to see Him in the situation and moving on her behalf.

Besides the rape, there were so many other experiences in Lena's childhood that caused her to have a distorted view of God. As a child, she would ask for the Sunday Comics section of the newspaper, but there was another section of the newspaper that she asked for and read daily. It was the Daily Horoscopes section. Even as a child, reading the horoscopes was just as normal to her as reading the Sunday Comics section. Lena remembered how her parents would often bring up her zodiac sign and would tell her this is why she did certain things, or was the way that she was. Her father and mother were in the habit of going to church, hardly ever missing a Sunday, and they made Lena go but Lena heard more from them about how astrology, not God, contributed to who she was. Truth be told, they never attributed any of who or how she was to God. She later realized that it was because they themselves did not know Him, or much about Him at all. Theirs was not a life experience with Him, only a Sunday-morning experience.

After she became a child of God through her belief and acceptance of Jesus as Lord, Lena found out church as she knew it as a child was so much different than she had come to know it as an adult. She learned that it was not just a place to go because her parents made her go or because it was a good way to start her week based on superstition. Yes, attending corporate worship service on Sundays is a very good habit and way to begin one's week, but not because doing so will help one to avoid trouble during the week just by going. No. What Lena learned is that doing so would help her to not avoid trouble but to get through any trouble that might present itself during the week – *in life.*

In corporate worship service is where she could worship the Lord shoulder-to-shoulder with other worshipers, each building the other up. It was also where she could have her faith added to and her mind renewed by the preached Word. She could also be equipped and empowered to go out and let her light so shine before men that they would see her good works and glorify the Father in Heaven. The equipping and empowerment that she got would also help her to weather any storm that might come along. She found that attending church has so many benefits, none of which included checking off an Attendance List.

Although Lena still goes to church because she has to, it is not the kind of "has to" where she is made to do so against her will. She goes because she has deferred her will for God's will and that in doing so, she is following in Christ's footsteps. Turns out, He was also in the habit of regular synagogue attendance. Lena realized that loving herself, loving and valuing her soul, means feeding it more than feeding her flesh; and

Signs

along with daily Bible reading and prayer, that corporate worship, Bible study, and fellowship were ways to do it. Lena also realized that she was not just going to church for herself but for others as well, to encourage them, even if only with a smile or a hug, and to provoke them toward love and good (God-like) works. She realized that just as He spoke to her one-on-one, and daily, that the Lord also had much to say in the corporate settings on Sunday mornings and on Wednesday nights. And, unlike the horoscopes that she read as a child, she also found that God's credibility was good every time He spoke. His Word is unfailing.

As she worked through her issues, Lena was thankful for that, and that God had never turned His back on nor forsaken her. He had to forsake Jesus, His only begotten Son, when He hung on the Cross and took rape and all the sins of humanity upon Himself in order that He could make and keep that promise to her. "I will never leave you nor forsake you." Lena never blamed God for what was done to her. As a born-again believer, she understood that in His power, God could have stopped it from happening. She also understood that this was what her parents were for. God needed vessels, and they were those vessels. They were supposed to protect her and keep her safe. They were supposed to have discernment to pay attention to the red flags regarding their friend. But how? After all, he was the same family friend who on Saturday evenings went to their home and got drunk with her parents and cussed with every other word out of his mouth it seemed. He was also a leader in their church who prayed the same rote prayer before the congregation Sunday morning after Sunday morning for as long as Lena could remember. The night that he raped her, Lena's parents had gotten so drunk that they passed out. After they passed out, he made his way into her bedroom, and.... She realized as an adult that there was no way that her parents could have seen the red flags concerning him because they were just as much a danger to her as he was by the religious, Christian-only-on-Sunday-mornings lives that they lived.

The abuse only happened once, because in an effort to protect herself, Lena thought to lock her bedroom door and pile things in front of it when he came over. He had attempted once or twice again to get into her bedroom, but the little fortress that she had built for herself seemed to be impenetrable. Lena eventually forgave her parents, especially after realizing that they did the best that they could to raise her with what they had, a lack of understanding of God. It is not to say that they could not have had more understanding though. Their ignorance of God, His Word, and their responsibility as parents were due to them not working out their self-professed salvation with fear and trembling. She also realized that even with all the knowledge of God that they could possibly have that they could not have protected her from every danger. However, almost every Saturday night, they invited danger into their home and got drunk with danger. If they had had any knowledge of and fear of God, there is a strong possibility that they would not have welcomed him in. Always looking for a Romans 8:28 in things though, Lena knew that somehow even the rape (yes, even the rape) and her parents' ignorance were being worked together for the good by God because she loves Him and is the called according to His purpose. The very fact that she had had enough fortitude to build that fortress at such a young age and that she is now healed and whole points to Jesus, His power and glory, and the truth that He is her Fortress.

Lena also forgave her offender. Several years after he raped her, he was arrested for the molestation of another child in the Church. Thankfully, that child's parents had close relationships with God, as well as with their child. So, when the child told them that he had touched her wrong, they believed her.

Another revelation that Lena had gotten as an adult and especially as a born-again believer, regarding her childhood, is that superstition and witchcraft are rampant in Christian churches and homes. As a young child, and especially in a "Christian" household, she should never have been allowed to read the horoscopes, but she followed the examples of those with the most influence in her life, her parents. Sure, her parents taught her the cute "now-I-lay-me-down-to-sleep" nighttime prayer as a child, but they never taught her that she could talk to God unceasingly and seek Him concerning every aspect of her life, no matter the time of day. She also learned that the only Mediator between her and the Father is Jesus–not a man, not an astrologist, not a palm reader or psychic, not a witch, and not even a deceased relative, but Jesus.

As harmless as it may seem, Lena realized that reading horoscopes was anything but.

Lena relied on them so much that when meeting new "love" interests, she would always ask them at some point, "What's your sign?" If their zodiac sign was incompatible to hers, or their stars did not align, or if her horoscope warned her against the person, it was a deal breaker for Lena. She learned to ask that from her mother, who always asked Lena's prom dates or boyfriends that question. It was sheer witchcraft!

Jesus said, "You shall know the truth, and the truth shall make you free," and Lena's deliverance from following astrology and practicing witchcraft came when she was in a Bible Study one night. The Bible account that they were studying was about King Saul when he went to the witch of Endor and had her summon the dead prophet Samuel's spirit. What stood out most to Lena was that the king disguised himself and the witch's reaction when she found out that it was the king who was patronizing her services.

It scared the witch to know that it was the king, because by all accounts, she should have been expelled from the land and, by his decree! Somehow, she had escaped, and she became afraid for her life upon realizing that it was King Saul who inquired of her. More than it was King Saul's decree to expel those who practiced witchcraft from the land, it was God's. Their practices were evil and He did not want the children of Israel consulting them for answers. Not only were they seeking out witches, but they were consulting with the dead through necromancers, with astrologers, and with ventriloquists and familiar spirits. God ordered that all who practiced those evils be banned, and that sorcerers be put to death. Because He is a jealous God and had created His people, He wanted only that they consult with Him regarding their lives. The practical application that Lena took from it was that it was like taking an import to a domestic car repair shop for issues that only the manufacturer of the import could repair. That domestic car repair shop might be able to do simple maintenance or repairs, but they could also cause more harm and open the door to more-costly repairs.

After becoming a Christian and a student of God's Word, Lena saw that she relied on the horoscopes most in the one area where she had sustained the most damage… love (as she once knew it to be) and relationships. She could only imagine the number of good guys she had not given a chance because of their zodiac signs being incompatible with hers. It was no surprise to God though, and she believed that there was a Romans 8:28 even in that. Had she held on to any one of those guys and married him, she would not have had this opportunity for a relationship with Jason, a God-fearing man. Worse yet, she might have turned down the invitation to be in a right relationship with God. The thought of that made her shudder.

One day as Lena was having lunch with a Christian co-worker, who attended a different church than her, she decided to tell the co-worker about Jason. She told her about how she believed that he was the answer to her prayers and about how much he loves the Lord. However, despite all that she had told her, her co-worker's response was, "So, what's his sign? You know you should find that out before this thing goes any further. No sense in wasting your time or his if y'all aren't compatible. Then, there are those trust issues that you struggled with in your last relationship." She then rolled her eyes and looked away as if to say that Lena was a hopeless case.

Lena could not believe what she was hearing. This woman was the Unmarried Women's Ministry leader at her church. In that moment, Lena…

FINISH IT!

Juanita E. Davis

READ

Bible verses that were referenced in the chapter:

- 1 Samuel 28:3-13
- Psalm 18:2; 22:1; 121:2
- Matthew 5:8, 16; 18:10; 27:45-46
- Luke 4:16
- John 1:12; 8:32
- Romans 8:28
- Philippians 2:12-13
- 1 Timothy 2:4
- Hebrews 10:24-25
- 1 John 4:7-8

Bible verses to consider when finishing this story:

- Psalm 1:1-3
- Leviticus 19:31; 20:6-8, 27
- Deuteronomy 18:9-14
- Proverbs 27:6; 29:25
- 2 Timothy 4:2

FINISH IT!

Chapter 3

Holy Matrimony

"I'm troubled by what I just heard. There are people who have fought to get married. Yet, marriage is the very thing that some of God's own children fight to get out of and usually for no justifiable reason, except irreconcilable differences or incompatibility. I mean, we will fight so hard to get out of the marriage, but we won't fight for the marriage. Marriage is a holy institution that God Himself has ordained in order that from that covenantal (not contractual, because there is a difference) union of a man and a woman would come godly offspring. I know that the two of you sought God in prayer as well as through a multitude of godly advisors before you got married, because I was one of them. Y'all sure had me convinced that you loved one another and that you were willing to spend the rest of your lives together. You even told me that both of you knew that God had ordained your union. So, what after only eight months has caused you to want to just walk away from each other and your marriage? Have either of you been unfaithful to the other? Do either of you feel unsafe?"

Tina began to squirm in her seat, because she knew that it was not "both of them" who wanted to end their marriage. Bradley had begged her to stay, but she still walked away. She knew that if she said right then and there that she wanted to stay and try to make things work that he would receive her back with arms wide open. Marriage was hard though. Although some of her friends and family had told her that when she told them of her engagement, she did not realize how hard it was. Her answer to them was always, "With Jesus on our side, we'll be just fine." The spiritually correct answer of course. She loved Bradley and had since they were both in middle school.

They met at a youth Bible camp when they were both twelve-years old. From the moment that they met, they were friends. Bradley had even told her on the last day of camp, as they were saying their good-byes, that they were going to get married one day. She believed it too, and from that moment on, Tina dreamed of their wedding day. She realized soon after getting married that she had never dreamed of their life after the wedding day, though. Maybe, it was because she thought that every day thereafter would be just as blissful?

Tina knew from watching her parents' marriage dissolve that marriage takes work, but she felt that her own marriage would be different from theirs, because she and Bradley were both Christians. Soon after saying their "I do's," she found out that although they were saved and children of God, that they had some of the same arguments that her parents had experienced. Sadly, they handled them, and each other, pretty much the same as her unsaved parents had done, too. She and Bradley would go days without speaking to one another, but it was mostly her not speaking to him. Just like her parents, it was because neither of them would humble themselves to say two powerful words. "I'm sorry."

One source of contention between them was Tina's career and what would happen with it after they began expanding their family. Tina and Bradley both had their master's degrees and very lucrative careers. The problem was that Bradley had suggested that when they start their family, Tina should quit working and become a stay-at-home-mom. True, Bradley's income alone was more than enough to not only provide the usual household needs but also to sustain their current lifestyle. Tina was very open to the idea, but she was also very afraid to give up her career and her income. She was afraid because her mother and other women that she knew (even in the church) had done the same.

They had stayed home for years taking care of home and household, only to get a raw deal when their husbands decided that they wanted new wives, and sometimes new children, too. It took years for some of those women, including her own mother, to re-establish their careers. Some of them were not educated beyond high school, so it was even harder for them to find gainful employment. What made it even worse for some of them was that some of those husbands (even in the church) fought hard against paying alimony and child support. Worse than the financial aspects of it, it was the fact that the women had basically seemed to lose themselves in being those men's wives, only to be cast off. It was a position that Tina never wanted to find herself in, so any time that Bradley brought up the subject, she made it clear to him that she would not be quitting her job. As clearly and as firmly as she told him that, she never told him why and despite his constant urging to find out why she felt that way, she refused to tell him.

"Tina, what are you afraid of?" Her pastor's question interrupted her thoughts. Without waiting for her to answer, he continued. "It's clear that both of you love one another with a deep love. Just like any married couple, you have your share of things to work out and that's the process of the two becoming one. From what you both have told me though, the biggest issue that you deal with in your own strength, and leave God out of, is the issue of you becoming a stay-at-home mother. So, what are you afraid of, daughter?"

Bradley was looking at Tina with that same desperate look that she had seen many times before but this time, it was also hopeful. He was most likely hoping that if Tina would not tell him privately why she did not want to quit her job that maybe she would tell him in the company of their pastor. Tina knew that she had a good man, and good in the way that the Bible defines a good man. Everything about Bradley said that he had a relationship with Jesus the Father and that going to church on Sunday's was not just a ritualistic habit. He loved the Lord, and second to Him (and Tina would have it be no other way) he loved himself, *his soul*, and then her, with that same soul-deep love. Did he have flaws? YES! He would be the first to tell others that he does and even what they are, but he strove daily to be more like Jesus.

With her, he was gentle. He was never domineering towards her. Just like when he suggested that for the sake of stability for their household, she leave her job and become a stay-at-home mom when they start their family. The key is that he suggested it. Their very own pastor, whom they were receiving counsel from this very day, had taught them in pre-marital counseling that submission is not the husband lording and ruling over his wife or constantly telling her what to do. Most times, it is him making suggestions or decisions. At times, he honors

Holy Matrimony

her suggestions, since submission can go both ways. Tina had no problem deferring her opinion to Bradley's, except giving up her career.

Bradley was very successful in his profession, and God was continually blessing him in it. It was apparent that not only did he have the Lord's favor, but also the favor of man when it came to his career. Therefore, Tina was not afraid that if he was the sole bread winner that they would suffer, nor that if he happened to die that she would struggle. Bradley Wright had his affairs in order even before they married, and he added to his portfolio afterwards. Again, her fear was that one day, he might decide to move on and erase her and any children that they might have not only from his financial portfolio, but also from his life. She knew that with her credentials and skills that should he erase her from his financial portfolio, that although she would have to start near the bottom, she could easily acquire another job in her career field. Starting over in her career was not a huge concern for her. Her bigger concern was the thought of being rejected and cast off by him. She was not willing to take that chance. Sadly, in her mind, her career was more of a guarantee and a constant to her than Bradley. That is why she was holding onto it, not because she loved it more.

Although she had not dreamt of life after their wedding day, Tina could think of no one else that she wanted to spend her life with and to be the father of her children. Bradley was all and more that she wanted and even needed in a husband; so, she knew that he would be a wonderful father. Again, he was not a perfect man, but just as he strove daily to be perfected, developed, and made like Christ, in life and in marriage, she had no doubt that this same attitude would carry over into fatherhood. She looked forward to becoming a mother, and the idea of being a stay-at-home mom was an honor. It had even become a dream of hers after she and Bradley got married, but as is the case with all dreams, you eventually wake up. Her wakeup happened when she told her mother of her plans, and her mother took care to remind her of her own experience and of other women in her family. Rejection hurts, and she did not want to hurt like her mother had, *or rather still was.*

Not every woman Tina knew that had either quit her career or put it on hold until her children became school-aged had been abandoned by their husbands. Tina knew that. In fact, she knew more who had not than who had, but they were not her mother or her aunts or other women whom she had close familial ties with. There were many women, to include her pastor's wife, who went from a career, to being a stay-at-home mom to her children, to full-time ministry once her children had all graduated high school. Her plan had been to go back into the workforce after their youngest child started grade school full-time, but she and her husband believed that God had other plans. Did they have to go without luxuries or, at times, have reason to worry about finances? Yes. They did, but her husband, who was still working a full-time occupation would often tell her, "Stay where you are, because with the help of the Lord; one day, I'm gonna be where you are. Let me work toward retirement, and when it happens, we can both devote more time to the Lord, to each other, and to the ministry."

By faith, Tina's pastor was able to retire at the age of fifty. Now, he and his wife are free to go when God says to go, or when they just want to get away together alone or to visit family and friends.

Holy Matrimony

There were other women in her church and in the Church community who had similar testimonies; but in her biological family, hers was the only marriage that was surviving, but barely it seemed.

Tina knew that Bradley was a different man than her father or any of the other men who had abandoned their wives, their children, and in some cases, even God. She also knew that it was foolish of her to allow fear any power in her life. It was hurting Bradley, it was hurting (not to mention, tormenting) her, and it was hurting others, God above all else. She loved Bradley enough that she was willing to give him the freedom to be able to marry someone who would be willing to give up the security of her career to become a stay-at-home mom.

Several days after Bradley's and her first counseling session with their pastor, a courier dropped off an envelope for Tina at her office. It contained the divorce papers. She had had her attorney draw them up the day before the session with their pastor. In fact, that is why they had the session. She told Bradley that she had seen a lawyer and that they would be getting the papers to sign soon. Hoping that it would change things, he asked if they could meet with their pastor. It did not. So, Tina didn't cancel her request to have the papers delivered to her at her office. She would sign them and then have them delivered by courier to Bradley at his office.

As Tina was taking the papers out of the envelope, with pen in hand and ready to sign them, she clearly heard in her heart, "What God has joined together, let no man put asunder." At first, she ignored it. However, as soon as she put pen to paper, she heard it again. In that moment, Tina… FINISH IT!

Juanita E. Davis

READ

Bible verses that were referenced in the chapter:

- Malachi 2:11b and 15
- Matthew 19:6
- Mark 10:9
- Ephesians 5:22-33

Bible verses to consider when finishing this story:

- Psalm 1:1-3
- Proverbs 3:5-8; 11:14
- Ephesians 5:22-33
- Philippians 4:6-7
- 1 John 4:18

FINISH IT!

Chapter 4

For Better or For Worse?

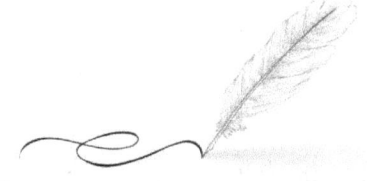

Melinda just sat there staring at the screen. She was in shock over what she was seeing. For a moment, she wondered if she could be hallucinating, but what she was seeing really was there on the screen. It was a direct message to her husband from another woman, and it revealed that her husband was possibly having an affair with the woman; if not sexual, then emotional at least. Melinda wondered which was more harmful though, a sexual affair or an emotional one.

Melinda and Harold had been married for almost twenty years, and in that time, she had never had reason to check his phone or his computer for "evidence." Harold was a good man who loved the Lord and her and up until this moment, she believed him to be a faithful man, as well. The only reason that she was on his tablet was because he had given her permission to electronically sign documents from their realtor, which had a short suspense. Since he had to work in the field that day, he asked her to sign the documents on his behalf.

As Melinda was scrolling through Harold's e-mails, looking for the one from their realtor, she noticed that he had an e-mail alert for a new direct message in one of his social media accounts. Normally, she would have scrolled past it, but in the subject line of the notification she saw the name of a woman that she did not recognize. Although she was tempted to open the e-mail and read it, Melinda looked for the e-mail containing the electronic documents and signed them. The documents were for a house that she and Harold were buying; and because she had already signed hers the day before, Harold's signature was the only one that was required to get the deal going. After signing it though, Melinda wondered if she should have. In light of discovering what she did, was there even a future for them? Buying another more expensive house could only make things more complicated if she and Harold were to divorce.

Theirs was not a perfect marriage. However, in the almost twenty years that they had been married, plus the two years that they had dated, none of their problems had been about either of them stepping out on the other. "So, why now," Melinda asked no one in particular. "Why would Harold decide now that he wanted to be with someone else?" Curiosity got the best of Melinda, so she decided to do some sleuthing. She and Harold shared almost everything, even their login credentials to social media apps, their devices, and e-mail accounts. She logged in to the app that the notification was from. The message read, "Thank you so much for yesterday. I really needed a shoulder to cry on." The woman followed it up with a hug emoji. Harold had yet to reply to the message, but the woman had only sent it a day ago; and with him working in the field, he probably had not seen the notification yet. Melinda found it strange that the two were not friends on the app though.

Melinda decided to log out of Harold's account and look the woman up through her own social media account. Since they were not friends, the woman's personal information was very limited. There was not much information to go on, but Melinda did notice that the woman looked very familiar. She just could not remember where she had seen her before. She could see that she was married with children and that she was quite homely looking, not quite Harold's type. However, Melinda did not let that deter her from thinking that her husband could be cheating on her, because she knew that some men cheated no matter how beautiful or not-so-fair-to-look-at the other woman might be.

Being a woman who turned a lot of men's heads, but also a woman who had been scorned in a past relationship by a cheating fiancé, Melinda knew that a woman's outward looks had little to do with keeping a man, or even at times getting one. She had respected her ex-fiancé so much that she had lost herself in him, leaving very little room for self-respect. She had worshiped him. He took advantage of her because of it, too, and she thought that she would never recover from their breakup and the fact that he had cheated on her. That relationship was not one that honored God, and Melinda knew it. She was saved. He, it turns out, was not. She was abstinent and waiting. He, it also turns out, was not, although he told her that he was. There are those with character, and there are characters. He was the latter. She saw the red flags, but he respected her relationship with the Lord and most of her Christian values. He just at some point stopped respecting her. However, because he had a lot materially and financially to lose if he broke it off with her, he played along, that is until Melinda found out about the other woman and bowed out of the game and his life.

After the breakup, Melinda did recover, and she realized that the breakup was one of the best things that could have happened to her. Through studying and applying the Scriptures, she grew and matured even more. She learned how to have a healthy respect for others without losing herself in the relationships, whether they were relationships with men, friends, or even family. She also learned how to view men from the proper perspective and not worship them. Before that breakup, Melinda did not know her worth, nor did she fully know who she was. As she began to grow in the knowledge of Christ, she also began to learn more about her worth and who she was in Him. It was because of this experience that she was able to have the utmost respect for Harold without losing herself in him or worshiping him.

She respected him so much that some of her extended family members accused her of worshiping him. "If only you all had seen me with my ex-fiancé—now **that** was worship," Melinda would often respond to her accusers. No matter how much she denied it though, they continued. So, she eventually gave up, reasoning that carnal minds can't understand spiritual things. The family members who accused her were other females. They were also either married and not submissive to their own husbands or had never been married, and if any professed to be Christians, it was mostly in name only. Her priorities were in the correct order: Worship the Lord and respect her husband. She knew that if anybody was to speak well of her husband and to do him no harm, that she needed to be first on that list. By honoring Harold, she was also honoring God. Sometimes, that might look to those who do not understand as if the wife is worshiping her husband. That is why some do not understand when they read in the Bible that Sarah called Abraham, lord. Biblically, there is a thin line between the respect that a wife should have for her husband and her worshipful regard for the Lord, and Melinda now clearly understood that this line was not to be crossed, nor blurred.

She had discovered that a woman respecting her husband is like stroking his ego, and there were many times where she would playfully call Harold her *Hercules*. Emotionally, it did something for him, as it does all men when their egos are stroked. It builds them up, and God knew that when He inspired the writer to tell women to respect and submit to their own husbands. She loved looking for ways to stroke Harold's ego just to see him blush in that kind of Gomer Pyle, "Aww, shucks," kind of way that he did when she "sang" his praises. What she hated though was the thought of another woman making him blush like that.

Rather than concoct her own narrative for what was going on, especially based on her past, Melinda decided to give her husband the benefit of the doubt and to pray. This was her only day off, and she still had housework that needed to get done, and it had already been delayed upon finding that e-mail. She was also really having to practice self-control, because her flesh wanted to keep digging and to even call Harold at work with the barrage of questions that she had for him. That would not be wise though, so she turned on Gospel music and started cleaning. Every now and then, thoughts of her husband even possibly having an affair and the pain that accompanied those thoughts would interrupt the good, true, noble, just, pure, lovely, virtuous, and praiseworthy thoughts that Melinda was striving to have while cleaning. At one point, she stopped cleaning and almost crumbled into a crying heap in the middle of her living room as she dusted picture frames, one of which held one of Harold's and her wedding photos.

Her ringing phone interrupted her pity party. When she saw that it was Harold, Melinda started to send the call to voicemail. However, if she did not answer, she knew that he would become worried and would just keep calling until she did answer. "How can he care so much for me that he would do that, but care so little for me that he would cheat on me," she thought. Before she answered the phone, Melinda cleared her throat and tried to mask the fact that she had been crying with a cheery tone. Knowing her as well as he did, Harold heard anyway and asked if everything was okay. Melinda told him that it was and left it there. Unconvinced, Harold kept asking until Melinda told him that something came up and that they could discuss it when he got home from work that evening. After she briefed him on the status of the paperwork for the realtor, Melinda told Harold that she needed to finish cleaning before it was time for her to pick up their children from school and ended the call. Their children. They had three children, and that was another thing that could complicate matters even more than they already seemed to be. Just the thought of how devastated they would be if she and their father divorced brought Melinda to tears once again.

As she sat in the carpool line waiting for her children to be released from school, Melinda saw a familiar face in another car that was on the opposite side of the street. "Could it be," she whispered to herself. It was *her*, and she suddenly remembered where she had seen the woman at before. Months ago, they had both chaperoned a field trip for one of Melinda's children and one of the woman's children, who were in the same homeroom. She did not recognize the woman's name in the e-mails nor on social media because when they met, the woman had introduced herself by what was apparently a nickname. The two women had gotten along very well on the field trip. They might have even exchanged contact information and kept in touch had things not been so hectic when they returned to the school. "But how does she know my husband, and why was she "crying on his shoulder" Lord," Melinda asked.

One thing that Melinda knew about extra-marital affairs was that some of them do not start out by a lust-driven man and woman deciding to have an affair. Some begin as friendships, where one or both "cry on the other's shoulder." In some cases, it is not about sex... not at first at least. Some affairs are emotional and are about one or both parties getting from outside of the marriage emotionally what they might crave or may be deprived of in their own marriage(s) or lives. For women, that is love and attention. For men, it is respect. If it happens at all between the two, sex is usually a result of the now-formed emotional bond. Harold was not deprived of neither respect nor anything else in their marriage, so what was really going on?

Just then, the woman got out of her car, crossed the street, and began to walk toward the school. She would have to pass right by Melinda's car. In that moment, Melinda shut off her car and reached for the door handle…

FINISH IT!

READ

Bible verses that were referenced in the chapter:

- 1 Corinthians 2:14
- Ephesians 5:22, 25
- Philippians 4:8-9
- Colossians 3:18
- 1 Peter 3:6

Bible verses to consider when finishing this story:

- Psalm 1:1-3
- Proverbs 3:5-8
- John 7:24
- 1 Corinthians 13:5
- Philippians 4:4-9

FINISH IT!

Chapter 5

To Give or Not to Give

"And that is exactly why I don't give all my money to the church," Vicky's roommate loudly exclaimed.

The two had been watching the evening news when a news story came on about their pastor. It seems that he was being investigated by the Internal Revenue Service as well as by local and other federal authorities for misusing church funds. Vicky was not surprised by the news because their pastor had told his version of the story at a recent Bible Study. He was very humble about it, and Vicky could tell that he was also very broken. His wife of almost ten years was right there by his side holding his hand, and sometimes squeezing it, as he talked. Based on her dealings with his wife, Vicky knew that she was doing more than squeezing his hand. She was also praying.

Pastor Erickson denied all allegations. He told those at the Bible Study that it was all a misunderstanding and that his name would be cleared. Though some doubted his story and made it very clear that night that they did, Vicky found no reason to doubt her pastor. He had been her pastor for the past three years, and she had never met more humble and genuine people than him and his wife. They were a lovely couple, and Vicky personally knew that they made a lot of sacrifices to help the congregation and the community. She knew from firsthand experience with them that before they gave from the church's finances that they would give from their own personal finances. That is why she believed that there had to be more to the story. Pastor Erickson was very vague when addressing the congregants though. She wished he had told more, and because he had not, Heaven's Gateway Church lost many more members that night.

"Vicky! Vicky! Are you listening to me?" Her roommate broke into her thoughts, and by the time Vicky heard her, she was pulling on Vicky's arm. "I asked you what do you think about this. Since you're close to his wife, has she told you anything? I can't believe that two people talk as much as y'all do and she hasn't said one word about it…" Vicky tuned her roommate out intentionally this time. She was having the conversation with herself, anyway, not giving Vicky room to get a word in edgewise. Besides, if her roommate knew anything about her, she should know that Vicky was not going to tell her or anyone else what she discusses with her pastor's wife. Since she was the church's Administrator, Vicky got that a lot—people wanting to befriend her to get information on the pastor. That was not the case with her roommate, but Vicky was still careful about what she told her, especially anything that she and Pastor Erickson's wife had discussed.

Vicky and Angela Erickson became fast friends upon meeting. Although they were the same age, that, and the fact that they both loved the Lord, was about all the women had in common. Two people could not have been any more different than they were. Angela (or "Lady Erickson") was a stay-at-home mom to two of the most adorable children that Vicky had ever met. Kasen was four years-old, Isabella was two years-old; and both being typical toddlers, they kept their mother quite busy. Although Vicky was the church's Administrator when the Erickson's came to Heaven's Gateway, she and Angela became close friends and prayer partners after Vicky began baby-sitting for them. The Erickson children would even spend weekends with her when their parents traveled out of town for speaking engagements. That is how much the Erickson's trusted Vicky. Angela once told Vicky that when she saw she could trust her with her children, that she knew she could trust her with her personal business because if she did not tell it, her children most certainly would.

Pastor Erickson was not only the full-time pastor of Heaven's Gateway Church, but he also owned and operated his own construction company, which was one of the largest construction companies in the tri-state area. Since the company was doing so well, the Erickson's had more than enough money to manage their own household. That is why the salary that Pastor Erickson earned from pastoring Heaven's Gateway all went back into the church and into the community around him. Pastor Erickson had only been the pastor of the church for three years, and in those three years, every idea of his to start an auxiliary to help the needy in the church and in the community was shot down by the Board of Trustees, which was led by the Associate Pastor. Seeing the trend of denials, Pastor Erickson prayerfully decided to receive the salary that the church paid him and to secretly give to the needy in the church and in the community from that, on behalf of the church. Sadly, many of those whom he had helped in the church left on the heels of the rumors.

Since his arrival and finding out about his business and personal wealth, people had complained that Pastor Erickson should not get a salary at all from the church, since he was a wealthy business owner. Pastor Erickson agreed with them wholeheartedly, but the impasse between the two sides was that where Pastor Erickson was getting a monthly check, the other side felt that he should not get one at all. Over the years, many came and left the church after those that remained and sowed discord got into their ears. One thing that Vicky's grandmother had taught her about a gossip is that in the Greek, a gossip means seed-picker like a crow. However, many times, gossips are only looked down upon for the messes that they leave, but hardly ever for the seed that they pluck up... the seed of the Word. Vicky and her roommate had many very passionate conversations about her roommate's tendency to gossip, and that is why Vicky had not told her roommate one word of what Angela had confided in her nor what Pastor Erickson had told her and a couple of the deacons after the Bible Study.

After her roommate and the larger group left the Bible Study, the night that he addressed the congregation, Pastor Erickson had shared with them that ever since he began receiving a salary, he had given every penny of it away. He went on to tell them that his reason for giving his paychecks away was not due to guilt for taking a salary, but that it was the only way to help the needy on behalf of the church since his idea for an auxiliary had always been rejected. Humbly, he showed them in the Word and in the church's bylaws that receiving a salary was his rightful due as a church leader. He told them that if the church had been struggling, he would not even accept the checks. It was not; so, he told God that he would accept them if He showed him whom He wanted to help with the money. With each check, Pastor Erickson honored the Lord by way of tithes and offerings, and then he prayed for the Lord's guidance on who from the congregation, or the community, needed help. The money never made it into the Erickson's household even though the bank account that the money was deposited into each month was a personal account. Although it never made it into their household, the Erickson's always reported it on their yearly income tax returns as income, as was expected of them both legally and morally. They knew that they could have used that money for groceries and other household needs, and then just used their personal income as discretionary money. However, they recognized his salary to be seed for sowing and not bread for consuming.

As her roommate continued to rant and rave about why she does not give to the church, Vicky was so tempted to tell her all that she knew up to this point to shut her up. She did not though, because it would have been her emotions driving her to do so and not the Holy Spirit leading her. Vicky knew that God was up to something, and she also knew that there was a part of the story that both Pastor Erickson and Angela (even Angela in their private conversations and prayer times had purposely left out. She truly believed that Pastor Erickson was innocent and that he could clear his own name if he would tell at least the Board of Trustees what he was doing with his salary. He would not though, and that was the part that made Vicky second guess his innocence. She felt guilty for it too, but it just did not make sense to her that he knew how he could clear his own name but would not. She knew that telling them what he does with his salary would not account for the missing funds, but it would at least show them his heart—that he was a giver and a man of integrity.

Being the church's Administrator, Vicky knew that she would get interviewed by the investigators. She was just as privy to the church's financial situation as the pastor and the Board of Trustees because she was the one that wrote the checks, Pastor Erickson's, the Associate Pastor's, other staff members,' as well as most of the checks for maintaining the building. The only check that she did not write was her own. It was written and signed by the Associate Pastor. She was no accountant, but Vicky had not seen where there were any major discrepancies. Some of the numbers were off here and there, but the Associate Pastor always told her when she questioned it that they were miscellaneous payments for things that usually did not come up every month. Outside of salaries and costs for maintaining the building, the church had no other financial obligations and was in a really good position financially. Pastor Erickson's vision was to add on to the building in the near future and to pay cash for the construction costs. Some of the members of the Board of Trustees made it clear that Erickson Construction would not be considered for the renovations, but Pastor Erickson was unmoved. Though their intent was to hurt him, he understood that it would be a conflict of interest for his company to do the work. Therefore, he never planned to bid for the job.

As Vicky was on her way home one evening, she noticed that a couple of lights were on at the church. There were no cars in the parking lot though. Assuming someone on the janitorial staff had forgotten to turn them off, she decided to stop in and turn them off. As she entered the wing where the offices and meeting rooms were, and where the lights were left on, she saw light and heard voices coming from the boardroom. Curiously, but cautiously, she walked closer to the door. It was slightly ajar, and just enough that she could clearly see that several members of the Board of Trustees, including the Associate Pastor and Deacon Fisher, were having a meeting. It was quite shocking to see them. Especially shocking was the fact that it was not the entire Trustee Board and that

To Give or Not to Give

Deacon Fisher, who was one of the ones that Pastor Erickson had confided in, seemed to be leading the meeting. No one had asked her to block the room off for a meeting, and if there was a special occasion like the pastor's birthday, anniversary, or some other event coming up it would not seem so strange. The fact that no one had contacted her and that there were no cars in the parking lot made it appear that it was a secret meeting that they did not want Pastor Erickson to know about. But why? The door was also ajar enough for Vicky to record the scene with her phone, so she began to record it just in time to hear Deacon Fisher speaking.

"Well, what do we do now," Deacon Fisher asked the group. "There is no way that he could be stealing money, especially after what he confided in me and a couple of others after Bible Study the other night about what he does with his salary. Every penny has come right back into this church and into the community." Then, looking squarely at the Associate Pastor, he said, "And that night, I figured out what all of this is about. That man, that true man of God, obviously knows that you're behind all of this, yet your name never came out of his mouth. I knew that he was withholding something, because why else would he not just go to the entire Board of Trustees **and** the authorities and tell them how he's been giving his salary away since he started receiving it? Some of the same people that have walked out and slandered him to anybody who would listen are some of the same ones that he helped with that money!"

At this, Vicky thought to herself, "Okay, so it wasn't just me thinking that Pastor Erickson was withholding information that could clear his name."

"You had us all convinced that the pastor was misusing funds when it's been you all along, moving money into a fake auxiliary account with a name that he presented, then using the money for yourself. All because he refused to not accept his salary and give it to you in the form of a raise instead? Then, you concocted all this nonsense because you're determined to have his salary and his position regardless of who gets hurt, and I can assure you that many already have been. This makes me sick to my stomach, and I pray that the good Lord will forgive me for ever having anything to do with this nonsense!" By this time, the deacon was crying but was also clearly very angry. Vicky could see that his fists were balled up and that he seemed to be contemplating whether he should punch the Associate Pastor. Just as quickly as he stepped toward the Associate Pastor though, he stopped and told him, "You're not even worth it. God is angry enough with me, and I won't hurt Him or anybody else any more than I already have. I'm going to pray for your soul instead."

As Vicky replayed the video now for the millionth time it seemed, she wondered if she should go to the Erickson's with it. They had been hurt enough, and she agreed with the deacon that they had to already know. Pastor Erickson and Lady Erickson obviously trusted God enough to patiently wait for the truth that he was being framed to bear itself out without them having to out the Associate Pastor. Ironically, as dirty as he was, he was also still God's anointed; and like David with King Saul, Pastor Erickson had great respect for the anointing that was on the Associate Pastor. She felt as though she was supposed to drive by the church that night. But, why? Why did someone forget to close the boardroom door all the way? Leaving it ajar just enough for her to not only see in but to also record footage with her mobile phone. As far as she knew, that video might not even be admitted in court if the case went that far. So, why? There was only one way to find out…

As the phone rang on the other end, Vicky's heart was pounding, and she was certain that she could hear every thump that it made and that the person she was calling would be able to, as well. When the person on the other end answered, Vicky began, "Uh, Deacon Fisher, this is Vicky…" She went on to tell him what she had seen and overheard at the church. At the end, she asked him if he would be willing to go to the authorities and even the media to clear Pastor Erickson's name. In response to a very long silence, Vicky told him that she knew that he was afraid because of what he had done before finding out the truth. She went on to tell him that she now understood why the Associate Pastor just explained away the discrepancies that she had seen in the church's financial records. In an attempt to calm his fears, she assured him (without telling him about the video) that he should be able to get a plea deal if charges were brought against him as well.

There was a very long silence, and then Deacon Fisher spoke, "You know, Vicky, I'm very sorry. Even though I now know that Pastor Erickson is innocent, I can't do that. I have repented to God for my involvement in this, but I would be risking too much if I went to the authorities and told them everything. I would incriminate myself, and I'm not willing to take that risk. Besides, Pastor Erickson is a man of faith, and I believe like he does that the Lord will clear his name."

As he finished speaking, Vicky was screaming on the inside, "But you have all the answers that will clear his name! What if God wants to use **you**?" Deacon Fisher then told Vicky to keep the faith and to have a good night. He then ended the call before Vicky could say another word.

In that moment, Vicky opened the video app on her phone, clicked on the video, and…

FINISH IT!

Juanita E. Davis

READ

Bible verses that were referenced in the chapter:

- Deuteronomy 25:4

- Isaiah 55:10b

- 1 Corinthians 9:9, 13-14

- 1 Timothy 5:17-18

Bible verses to consider when finishing this story:

- Psalm 1:1-3

- Esther 4:14; 7:5-6

- Luke 8:17

- Romans 16:17-18

- James 4:17

FINISH IT!

Chapter 6

Birthing Greatness

Scarla replayed her mother's words over and over in her mind. She was at a crossroads, and as usual she went to her mother for advice. Her mother was a spiritually mature Christian, who clearly loved the Lord and others. When Scarla went to her for advice and prayer, she would sometimes forget that it was just her mother that she was talking to. That was because as she got older, Scarla and her mother became close friends; and the conversations with her mother were always a sharpening for her. Scarla sometimes jokingly referred to her mother as her "Paulette," or her spiritual mentor, as the Apostle Paul was to Timothy and others. Her mother was very objective and never hesitated to tell her the truth, even if it hurt. She told Scarla that because she loved her to Life that she would rather wound her with the truth than to deceive her with kisses as an enemy of her soul would do.

When she talked to her mother the night before, Scarla had called her about a decision that she had been entertaining for quite some time. She had been attending a smaller church since its inception. The church was about five years-old, and Scarla was starting to feel that her friends were right when they told her that she needed to attend a bigger church. After all, they all had left "Small Church" to attend bigger churches. "But they're always coming to **you** for prayer and advice, Scarla. So, what are they getting from those churches besides bragging rights," her mother once asked her. Her friends were not very active in their churches, and a couple of them were no longer attending church anywhere. Going to bigger churches of well-known pastors only seemed to give them bragging rights, as her mother had said. After a year or two of attending Small Church, they got antsy and went in search of bigger. One of her friends even told Scarla, "You have greatness in you that needs to be birthed out, and I don't think you can get it at a smaller church. God has given you gifts, and He desires that you use them. You're just sitting on them there. That's why I left."

"Greatness in you that needs to be birthed out of you is not so much about your gifts as it is about your character, dear," her mother told her. "Oftentimes, that's where younger Christians get it wrong. They put the *do* before the *be*. Yes, God cares about both, but we can't put the cart before the horse, and that's what we often do. When the Word tells us to be doers of the Word and not just hearers only, it's talking about our be-*ing* about the Word and living it, and not necessarily about us just exercising our gifts. Selfish ambition is a real thing, and it is sadly very prevalent in the Church. It leads many astray in that they think that because they can do something well, like teach, sing, play an instrument, preach, etcetera, that they're done and ready to come off the potter's wheel and lead others. That's deception, and many have fallen away because of it. One thing my mama used to say to me, and your aunts and uncles often is, "If you tell me that you're grown enough to do it, then you're not grown enough. She was alluding to that pride and arrogance that we had," Scarla's mother said with a chuckle.

Her mother went on to tell her to look at the lives of the friends who were advising her. She was always careful not to speak against them, and Scarla never told her which of her friends had advised her at any given time. Her mother always guessed though, because when her daughter was in high school, many of them spent lots of time at their house. Some of them were like her own children. "Look at So-and-So. She left Small Church because it was too small, according to her. Then, she went over to a bigger church, and was immediately placed in a position of leadership because her gift of singing was recognized. It seems that no one took the time to get to know her and to discern that she was not ready for that much responsibility. Could she sing? Yes! Was she ready to lead a choir? What we must understand is that the gifts are already developed. It is the carrier of the gift that needs to be developed. So, she got there, and people were loving her singing, even coming just to hear her sing; but then the other choir members began to hate her because she was a novice leader – arrogant and talking down at them. Once the pastor began to get complaints and people began to quit the choir, he asked her to leave the choir because she was not a good fit for it. He didn't even give her the option of remaining on the choir. He, the one who laid hands on her too quickly, just totally dismissed her. Now, she's hurt and is not going to church anywhere, and you're taking advice from her?"

What her mother said was so right. Her friend, who was the main one encouraging her to leave Small Church, wanted nothing to do with church anymore. Life as she knew it had become messy and unlike what it was when she was attending Small Church. Her passion for God was gone. When she was attending Small Church, she was growing and thriving from within, and she had a genuine desire to know God. Her disgruntlement came about with the pastor of Small Church because he would not allow her to form a choir. His reasoning was that it was not time. Her reasoning was that if they had a choir, they might get more people to come and join the church. The pastor, being a man of God, stood his ground though. He explained to her that he more than she, or anyone else, wanted the church to grow, but that they had to all grow and develop inwardly first. There was no doubt that their pastor heard from God and that he spoke for God, but her friend, in the case of the church forming a choir, felt that she was the one hearing from God about when to form a choir and that their pastor was not. So, she left.

"Greatness was birthed in a stable, Scarla," her mother had told her. "Surrounded by stinky animals and lacking the proper staff, let alone a midwife to birth the baby. God didn't make reservations at nor ordain that His Son be born in a palace or even in an inn. There wasn't even a midwife on standby. Greatness, the baby Jesus, was born in the most unlikely place and by the unskilled-for-delivering-a-baby hands of a carpenter, His earthly father Joseph. Just like you and me, Jesus had to learn right from wrong as a child, and He, too, had to be prepared for His ministry. Could He teach? Better than any, but He also had to mature and to develop – to grow in wisdom, stature, and in the favor of God, AND man. God, the Creator of man and all things, the Beginning and the End, came to the Earth and experienced something that was a first for Him. A flesh suit. A body and all the emotions and the temptations that came with it. Because of that newness, He too had to learn to subdue the flesh and all of its sinful tendencies, and He succeeded.

Birthing Greatness

That's what character building is like, subduing the flesh and walking after the Holy Spirit. And how long did it take for Him to be prepared for His ministry? Yet, we want to rush out as soon as we hear the call from God—unprepared!

So many have walked away from the very ministries that the Lord planted them in, not the most ideal places by their standards, or others,' but the places where they were intended by God to flourish and to bear fruit in old age. The Lord knows what it will take to give birth to greatness in each of us. We need to let Him be the Planter. It gets me how we'll use Proverbs 3:5-6 for where we'll shop for groceries, but we won't acknowledge the Lord when looking for a church home.

I have nothing at all against larger ministries. I don't have to convince you. Your own father is a world-renowned pastor and leader of a big church. He wasn't always that though, and you know that. You were there in the beginning. The doors were like revolving doors, and we wondered if the ministry would ever grow. Those were some very discouraging days – *years* – for me, for us, but God. Early on, He told me, "Your small is big," and I realized that I had to say about the church what He said about it, and I had to see it before I saw it. Almost twelve years into the ministry, God showed me how time is His filter and that time, or rather, waiting, is the problem with many of His children. Not only are we fickle, but we can be impatient too. SO impatient. I can't tell you what to do, but I will tell you this. Small Church is blessed to have you, and you it. It's going to see outward growth in that more and more people will began to come and will stay, but y'all must grow and mature inwardly first or the outward growth might take y'all out. The core must be strengthened first, or y'all won't be able to withstand what's coming. Just like with your father's church in the early days, there will even be some who will come saying that God sent them. The test for their words and what's really in their hearts – God's agenda or their own hidden ones – is time. Let time run its course, beloved.

The best encouragement that you can be for your pastor, and not just him but for his wife, his family, and others, is to be there. Just be there; and by "be there," I mean all in, not you there physically but in your mind longing to be somewhere else. In the same way that you're tempted to leave, and that others have been and did, do you not think that your pastor and his wife have been tempted to quit also? There were many times that your father and I were, but we had to be steadfast, unmovable, always abounding in the work of the Lord… knowing that our work was not in vain in the Lord. The problem that I see far too often in the Church is that the saints don't exercise staying power. Oh, we have it, because God gave us that with Holy Spirit and His full armor. Rarely, do we exercise it though. The apostle Paul knew that far too well, when he wrote to the Church at Ephesus asking that they pray for him and all the saints. Before that request, he told them to put on the whole armor of God, so that they could withstand the fiery darts of the enemy, and having done all to stand. No one without roots, or even with shallow roots, can stand though. That's why it is so important to be rooted and grounded in Christ and in Him only.

You told me once that the advice from your friends is always unsolicited, and I believe you. However, if you are still having that same conversation with any of them, then it means that you're not shutting them down. That's not standing. You can stand your ground without shooting them down. There's a difference between shooting them down and shutting them down. The fact that you say nothing to defend your pastor or the church, a true prophet of God and a church that God clearly sanctioned, says that you might very well agree with them. Be careful, my dear. If you choose to stay at Small Church, ask the Lord to renew your mind and to help you stand. And whatever that might look like to your friends, whether it's changing the subject, speaking well of your pastor and church, boasting about God's goodness to the Church, rebuking them, or even telling Satan to get thee behind you, when they see you standing, they just might be humbled enough to return. Whether they return or not, they will be humbled enough to shut up, and they will know that they can't have that conversation with you anymore. Standing might even mean you cutting off communication with them. Whichever way Holy Spirit leads you to stand though, it will get them out of your ear. I'll be praying your strength in the Lord. I love you, and good night." With that, the phone call between Scarla and her mother ended.

As time went on, Scarla ended communication with many of those friends who tried to persuade her to leave Small Church. After witnessing her resolve, one of them even returned. There was, however, a friend that she could not avoid, because they worked in the same office. Scarla tried her best to avoid having long conversations with her, so much so that she began going to lunch at a different time. The two used to have lunch together every day, but Scarla changed her lunchtime the day after her conversation with her mother. She had made the decision to remain at Small Church, and she did not want others' negativity to cloud her judgment.

"Wait for me," Scarla heard someone yell from behind her as she was heading towards the break room. It was the office friend, who attended a bigger church and tried relentlessly to persuade Scarla to leave Small Church and come to the bigger church. Scarla pretended not to hear her as her co-worker power-walked to catch up with her and yelled for her to slow down. It did not matter if she waited for her or not, because it turns out that her office friend was headed to the break room for lunch as well. She had changed her lunch schedule for that day because she had a meeting in the afternoon.

"Ooh! You're making me work my lunch off before I even eat it, Scarla," her friend said laughingly as she caught up with her. Even before they could find a table and sit down in the break room, the negativity began, "So, what's been going on with you? Are you still at Small Church? Girl, my church is growing so much that they're having to get a bigger building. You should have been there Sunday! My pastor brought the house down with his sermon. I keep telling you that you need to come on over there. What about Small Church? Have y'all grown any?"

In that moment, Scarla stopped, turned around, looked her co-worker squarely in the face, and…

FINISH IT!

Juanita E. Davis

READ

Bible verses that were referenced in the chapter:

- 1 Kings 12:6-19

- Matthew 16:23 and Mark 8:33

- Luke 4-7

- 1 Corinthians 15:58

- Ephesians 3:14-21; 6:10-20

- 1 Timothy 1:2; 2:22

- Hebrews 10:2

Bible verses to consider when finishing this story:

- Psalm 1:1-3; 92:12-15

- Nehemiah 4:1; 6:1-5

- Proverbs 4:23; 6:19b; 26:4-5

- Micah 5:2

- Zechariah 4:10

- Ephesians 6:10-18

- James 1:19-20

FINISH IT!

Chapter 7

By Faith

The Bible study leader continued, "It will require faith and confidence in the Lord to do it. Confrontation is not easy, and one of the many problems in the Church is offense and the lack of resolve. Take *Sister Unstable.* She gets mad because she thought the pastor was talking about her in his sermon, and maybe he was, because he only said what the Lord gave him to say. Instead of confronting him about it, she talked to everybody in the church about him, left, and kept talking to others about him – those in the old church as well as her new church. And, yes, the new church. She left the old church citing the Lord told her to leave. Many times, what Christians do is make the Holy Spirit appear to be as emotionally unstable as we can sometimes be. God does not endorse nor promote division in His Body, and that is when we know that a person is either mistaken or lying on God when they say in one breath that He told them to come, and then in the next that He didn't.

Even perceived offenses need to be dealt with. Had *Sister Unstable* gone to her pastor and spoken with him, she would have found out that he knew nothing about her situation. A pastor once told me that one of his congregants and her mother, who was visiting, had left a worship service mad at him. The pastor had preached from Ephesians 5, which in part warns against sexual immorality, greed, and drunkenness, to name a few. The young lady's mother, who had her own reasons to be convicted, had convinced her daughter that the pastor's wife must have been on social media that Sunday morning and seen that the young lady had gone out the night before and gotten drunk. She then convinced her daughter that the pastor's wife had told her husband about the post and that he had based his sermon on that.

The young lady called the pastor later in the week to tell him that she was leaving the church. He asked her why, and she told him what her mother suspected. She also told him that she had not posted anything about her outing on social media. He told me that he later apologized to the young lady for his response, which was laughter. After he sobered up from laughing, he asked her, "So, you're telling me that your mother convinced you that my wife saw a non-existent post by you on social media where you said that you had gone out and gotten drunk? And that she then told me about it, and I built my sermon around that, that morning? You know it's the devil when there's absolutely no logic to it!" He went on to assure the young lady that he was not laughing at her but was instead laughing with the Lord at the wicked, based on Psalm 37:12-13.

By the time the young lady called the pastor, her mind was already made up to leave. Therefore, it was clear that her motive for calling was not for reconciliation; but the call did result in that, and she stayed.

By Faith

Sadly, many people would have left offended without making even that call. They would have avoided confrontation by saying that they would just pray about the situation. I would love to be a fly on the wall and hear how those conversations between God and them might go. It would have to be them doing most of the talking, because all I can imagine God saying is, "Do My Word." God, the Author of the Holy Bible, is unable to give counsel that contradicts His written Word and Who He is. Therefore, I can't imagine Him telling someone to do anything other than what it would take to bring about unity and/or personal Christian growth.

With that said, there are times that we won't be led to confront others. I say that because as a younger Christian, I was very sensitive and easily offended. One day, I had gotten offended by someone, and as I was talking to God about it, He told me to grow up! The Bible Study leader laughingly said, "I was so ready to go and confront the person. I just wanted God to tell me when, but instead, He told me to grow up." So, I say to each of you, let God check you before you wreck not only yourself, but others around you, as well. Matthew 18:15-20 is not for every little offense. Some things can be resolved easily between two people when both are humble and mature. Then, there are some things that don't need to be confronted at all, at least not with others but within us. That is why it is so important to walk after the Holy Spirit, because He will give us discernment to know when to confront and when not to.

As far as those times that we are to confront someone because they offended us, it can be a hard thing to do, but is there anything too hard for the Lord? That is where faith in Him comes in. Most of the time, it's hard for us because we don't trust Him as we should. Then, there's the fact that we don't want to be vulnerable and show our weakness especially to an offender. Bottom line, we don't confront due to fear. But whom should we fear more? The one who can only destroy the body, or the One who can destroy both body and soul? If we must take witnesses with us because our offender would not hear us the first time, then take them, and go in Jesus' name. After all, the result is for His glory and His renown, not ours. He has promised that He would be in the midst where two or three are gathered in His name. The principle of that promise is relevant for Sunday-morning gatherings, sure, but the primary reason for it was to encourage the offended and to convince them that they are not alone in the confrontation, regardless of the outcome.

Children of God, you've got to understand that our Father in Heaven hurts when two of His children are not getting along. After all, the love that we have for one another is how we identify as Jesus' disciples. Being the God of unity that He is, He's given us counsel in His Word on how to attain unity. He knows that sometimes hearts are so hardened that the offender might not hear us out. The sister might deny that she did anything wrong, or she might just brush it off and deem it water under the bridge. The danger in that though is that that water under the bridge is drowning both the offended and the offender, and more than likely others, if allowed to keep flowing..."

Mallory listened intently as the Bible Study leader spoke. She was dealing with a situation herself where she had gone to someone who had offended her. Twice, the person did not hear her out and instead said that it was in the past and that they should leave it there. It took a lot of courage for Mallory to even go to the person those times, and afterwards she just felt foolish and as though the person thought that she was just being sensitive. Mallory would pray about it, and she would be fine until the next offense. You see, her offender was a close family member.

By Faith

More than a close biological family member, she was also a fellow church member.

Deciding that she was going to ask for advice on how to deal with the family member, Mallory raised her hand. "Yes, Mallory, go ahead," the Bible Study leader said. Mallory shared with the group about how she had gone to her family member more than once to try to resolve their issues, but the family member did not hear her out. She also told them how the person was very competitive and had an attitude of whatever you can do, I can do better or whatever you have, I can have bigger and/or better. Mallory finished by telling them that over the years, many misunderstandings had gone uncleared between them and had begun to affect other relationships with her and others in their biological family and the church. Those relationships were affected, or rather infected, because the family member would try to get close to those whom Mallory was closest to, at the expense of smearing Mallory's name.

One of the other members, Tracy, spoke. "I once had a similar situation. The person was also a family member, but by marriage. She was also a professed believer, but she was very self-absorbed. She loved to talk about herself and her accomplishments, and any time someone shared a testimony, she would strive to one-up theirs with her own. It was as if she was trying to convince others that God loved her more than them. Sometimes, I would forget that He is no respecter of persons and would fall for the lie. I dreaded going around her, because being around her, especially when some of her allies (other family or church members whom she had turned against me) were with her, it would be like a scene from the movie *Mean Girls*. We both sang on the choir, but she had a clique on the choir. I tried to get along with all of the choir members, but it was apparent that she and some of them talked about me behind my back. Christians, y'all! I'm not talking about a bunch of pagan high-school girls but grown, so-called Christian women!

However, like Mallory, I prayed about it and decided that I was going to talk to her about it and to try to clear up the misunderstandings that were between us, and there were a lot. The first time I confronted her, she also swept it under the rug, saying that it was in the past. What she didn't see was that it was not in the past, but it was a big fat elephant that was always in the room every time either of the families, biological or spiritual, got together. Not only that, but that elephant was feeding off the issues and the misunderstandings between us and was only getting fatter and more powerful. But not more powerful than God. So, what I did was handle it the way that Jesus had prescribed in Matthew 18:15-20. Being that she and I also attended the same church, and our little rift was no secret and had spilled over at least onto the choir, I invited our pastor's wife and one of the older deaconesses to meet with us."

Mallory then asked, "But how did you get her to go to the meeting?"

"Oh, she put up some resistance at first, but I told her that it was not about me and her. The issue had to be resolved or else that poison was going to start to cause more damage in our family and in the Church, but mostly in each of us. We all met, and before we even began to speak about the issue, our pastor's wife led us in prayer. She pointed out afterwards that we were not gathered in anybody's name but Jesus' – not mine, not my relative's, not the church's. That set the atmosphere. I spoke first, and I told my family member all the same things that I had in our initial conversation. She was clearly getting a little hot-headed as I talked, and even tried to interrupt me a few times, but the deaconess quietly whispered to her, "You'll get your turn. Just hear her out." And she did. Her facial expressions were hard to read. At times, there was embarrassment, then anger, then some expressions that were just unreadable. After I spoke, she spoke; and she took ownership for the wrongs that she had done towards me and apologized. I even apologized to her, because there had been times where I got in my feelings and didn't handle things in a Christ-like manner. We both cried and hugged, and the meeting ended. Not all of the misunderstandings were cleared up, but I believe that the ones that needed to be were. Above all else, our Father in Heaven was glorified."

"Wow!" One of the other Bible Study attendees exclaimed. "In all my years in the Church, I have never actually seen Matthew 18:15-20 practiced. I have seen a lot of people fall out and leave the Church over offenses, and some of them even fell away from God. It just amazes me that people get hurt by people, but they blame God and fall away from Him."

"And," Tracy interjected, "I will add that my relative and I now have healthy boundaries. We realized that we might not ever be as close as we once were, but what we did regain for one another was respect, after the Spirit. As for the competition between us, it has ended. I tapped out of that competition long before the meeting. It's too costly. What I realized is that God can only change us if we allow Him to change us. He won't force change on us. Sadly, my family member has only changed her target. And until she allows God to deal with her insecurities, that's how it will be. That's the truth for all of us."

Tracy then looked directly at Mallory and said, "Call on trusted leaders in your church and ask them to meet with you and her. In my case, we didn't have to take it before the church, but be prepared to.

Jesus gave us three steps for a reason. Trust Him. It really does take faith in Him to confront someone knowing that sometimes, it might be like poking a sleeping bear and that they'll only get worse. But God. Go in the name of Jesus, Sister."

Mallory was nervous when she approached Cindy after church, that next Sunday. She had prayed and asked God for the opportunity to do so, and she believed that this was it. "Hey, Cindy, how are you?" The two women hugged, and she could feel eyes on them. A couple of the other members, or rather Cindy's allies who had been standing close by, moved in closer just in case Cindy… *needed backup?* Really? "Cindy, I was wondering if you would be willing to have a meeting with me and a couple of the church leaders regarding the unresolved issues between us…" Mallory began, but Cindy cut her off.

"Mallory, are you still on that? I've told you that there's nothing to talk about. It's the past."

In that moment, Mallory inhaled deeply, and…

FINISH IT!

Juanita E. Davis

READ

Bible verses that were referenced in the chapter:

- Psalm 37:1213

- Matthew 10:28; 18:15-20

- John 13:34-35

Bible verses to consider when finishing this story:

- Psalm 1:1-3

- Psalm 34:14b; 133:1-3

- Matthew 18:15-20

- 2 Corinthians 5:7

- Hebrews 11:1; 12:14-15

FINISH IT!

Chapter 8

Creator of All, Father to Some

I believe that if anyone could have asked God in the beginning what sized family He wanted, He would have smiled big, opened His arms wide, and replied, "This big!" The evangelist on T.V. went on to say that Jesus had done just that when He hung on the Cross.

With arms spread wide, the Son, the Seed, gave His life and died in order that God could add more sons (more children) to His family. Her message was from the Book of John 8:31-47, where Jesus was addressing the Jews who had once believed in Him. They were claiming to not only be Abraham's children, but ultimately God's. Jesus was clearly letting them know that because they did not love Him and were trying to kill Him that they were neither Abraham's nor God's children, but the devil's.

In His address, Jesus told His audience that their father the devil 'speaks his native language when he speaks, for he is a liar and the father of lies.' The evangelist then asked, "Why would Jesus bring that up about the devil, when the subject was about whether those Jews, who had once believed in Him, were God's children? I'll tell you why. It's because the popular saying of, "We're **all** God's children is a lie," the evangelist said very passionately. "It's a lie, and it goes all the way back to that conversation in our text. So often we hear, and I'm going to pick on Christians right now, that lie rolling off the tongues of Christians. It's a lie! Don't fall for the lie, y'all. God is Creator of all, but He is not Father to all. Hear me again, believers. God is Creator of all, but He is not Father to all. That's a hard teaching for many, because some of you sitting here in this room, or watching by television or the internet, may have just said, "We are all God's children," to someone to comfort them. God knows your heart. He knows that you meant well, but He would that none of His children remain in the dark. That is why you're hearing this message today."

Susan sat there stunned. She had never heard a teaching like this before, and she had heard her own pastor say, "We are all God's children," many times from the pulpit. Ignorantly, she had accepted it as truth, instead of searching it out in the Scriptures herself. Just weeks ago, she had heard a world-renowned religious leader say it to a worldwide audience during a televised speech. The evangelist that she was listening to right now was not very well-known. Her popularity paled greatly in comparison to the world-renowned religious leader and even to her own pastor, but there was something about her that made Susan want to pay attention to every word that flowed from her mouth—and to believe what she said, because she spoke as though God was speaking through her.

The evangelist was clearly a teacher of the Word and therefore backed up this current teaching and every teaching with verses from the

Bible, and not just one verse but many. Her husband, who was the pastor of the ministry, was the same way. Susan came across one of their recorded services while on a popular app one day. Although she had never heard of either of them, she was prompted by the Holy Spirit to stop scrolling and to listen to the message. For Susan, it was the start of something in her; and she could only describe it with one word, *Growth*.

After listening to the first sermon, Susan subscribed to the church's channel. She was not able to tune in to the live broadcasts, since her church met at the same time that it aired, but she never missed a message. On Sunday evenings, she would set aside time to tune in to that day's broadcast to hear what God was saying to her. That's always what it was like too – like God was speaking to just her through them. The messages were always timely. Sometimes, they contradicted some of what she had learned from her pastor over the years, but the couple always encouraged those in their congregation and those watching remotely to not just take their word, but to study the Scriptures for theirselves. Once Susan began to do that, any confusion that might have existed because of the two sometimes-different teachings was quickly cleared up with the new teaching always trumping the traditional and even wrong teachings of her pastor. Her pastor meant no harm. It was clear to Susan that he was mostly teaching what had been taught to him, and it was also clear that he was not studying the Scriptures. That was harmful to not only him, but to those he pastored.

At this point, Susan knew that Holy Spirit was not leading her to go join the pastor and evangelist's church, not yet anyway. So, she wondered what she should do with this new information.

One thing that she had already done was share the ministry's channel link with family members and friends, some of whom attended the same church as Susan. She hoped that somehow her pastor could get it too. In that same address to the Jews who had once believed in Him and thought that they were God's children, Jesus told them, "Then you will know the truth, and the truth will set you free." Susan was getting to know the truth, Jesus, through the online ministry, and she so wanted her pastor to get it too. She was quite tired of the strictly traditional and impure religious practices and teachings. She was hungry for truth, and she did not realize that she was hungry until she heard it. Getting it to her pastor though was something that she would have to pray about a little longer, because that answer was coming much slower than the leading to share the channel link with others had come. *Or was it?*

The Wednesday following the Sunday when she heard the message about God being Creator of all but not Father to all, the answer came; but not in the way that Susan had imagined. No. It was much better, and it was without a doubt by God's design. That night for Bible Study, her pastor had assigned one of the ministers, his son, Minister Tomkins, to teach, and her pastor was in attendance. The topic that Minister Tomkins spoke on was "Sheep and Goats," and he based the lesson on Matthew 25:31-46. After reading it, he said to those in attendance, "Being a sheep is comparable to being a child of God, whereas being a goat is comparable to not being a child of God." Susan was once again stunned, not so much by what the minister had just said but because she could see God all over this message, and she had not heard it yet. She was also stunned because she had not shared that link with Minister Tomkins nor with anyone who would have shared it with him.

Creator of All, Father to Some

When his son made his opening statement, Susan noticed that her pastor sat up in his chair as if his antennae had just gone up. Minister Tomkins, or rather GOD, had his attention. "We've often heard, or read, on the news or social media that a famous person has died, and then as part of the tributes we've heard or seen where others have said, "Rest in peace or rest in heaven, so-and-so." I'm not here to tell you who has gone to Heaven and who hasn't, but I can tell you what will keep us out of Heaven for eternity based on what God has said in His Word. Did not Jesus say that if you 'deny Me before men, that I will deny you before my Father?' Sadly, many have denied Jesus. So, if Jesus and His ways are strange enough to keep a person from believing in and receiving Him on Earth, why would that person even expect to live with Him for eternity? Strange, right?

Can you imagine a stranger coming to your door and ringing the doorbell and exclaiming, "I'm home," when you open the door? IF you open the door. You would most likely slam the door in their face. I know I sure would," Minister Tomkins exclaimed with a laugh. Sobering up, he continued, "Seriously, many have been misled, either through erroneous teachings or through blatant heresy. Only those who have believed in and received Jesus, those who have confessed or come into agreement with God that He is Lord and who believe in their hearts that He was raised from the dead, His children, will spend eternity with God. Spending eternity with God is a family affair, and if you are not a member of His family, His household, you don't get the privilege of living with Him forever. That brings me to my next question.

Does God send people to hell? The answer is, "No." Let's look at John 3:16-17. When God sent His Son Jesus to the Earth, He sent Him to save the world, not to condemn it. He couldn't condemn us because we were already condemned to spend eternity separated from God. We were all already on that bus, if you will, with hands and feet chained up, headed to hell. But because He loved us, because He had a social and moral concern for us, because He wanted to have a Father-child relationship with us and cared that we were sin-sick and wanted to heal us, God sent His Son to save us. He sent Jesus as the Seed that through His death, He would produce more seeds, or sons." Looking out over the room, Minister Tomkins asked, "I know that that's a lot, so do I have any questions before I go on?" At that, several hands went up, including Susan's.

"Yes, Susan," he said.

Knowing the answer, but being led to ask a question instead, Susan asked, "So, how does a person become a child of God?"

"You know, Susan, that's a good question. I'm glad you asked, but rather than answer it myself, I want to give someone else an opportunity to answer it. Anybody," he asked.

Immediately, the hand of someone whom Susan knew had watched the video link that she had shared raised her hand. After Minister Tomkins called on her, she shared that we become sons and daughters of God by believing in and receiving Jesus. She also went on to say that the moment that we believe in and receive Him that it is like going from foster children to adopted children with all the same birthrights as a biological child. In this case, it is Jesus whom we would share birthrights with. Susan could see that her friend had really paid attention to that message. Susan was in awe of God and how He was answering her prayer right then, that night, and in that Bible Study! Judging from the look on her pastor's face, he was very intrigued, and she hoped he was getting it.

After taking several more questions, Minister Tomkins began to wrap up the lesson. "In my opening, I stated that being sheep is comparable to being God's children and that being goats is comparable to not being His children. When Jesus returns and separates the two and puts the goats on His left and then sends them away to eternal punishment, let's understand that His sending them will only be Him respecting their decision to remain in condemnation. God sent His Son because He loved the world, and by "world" that means everyone. He gives us each a choice though. To believe or to not believe in His Son as being Lord. That is the choice that is before every man and woman, every soul.

Many are comforted by the false notion that they can live their lives however they want, separated from Christ on this Earth, and still somehow spend eternity with Him. That is not the case at all. Some believe that if they are good and never bother anyone, or if they do good works without ever acknowledging Christ, that they will somehow spend eternity with Him. Let me tell you this. If your goodness doesn't point others to Christ, then it's not good enough. That's your righteousness, and to God it's as filthy rags. As far as works, no one can work their way into Heaven. No one. Man's goodness nor his good works can get him into Heaven. Jesus is the only Way to God and us having that Father-child relationship with Him. After life on Earth is over for every person, we will each see God. The question is, will we see Him as God and Father and spend eternity with Him? Or will we see Him as God and Judge only and spend eternity separated from Him?" Susan noticed that her pastor began to move about in his chair as if he were uncomfortable, but she did not know if it was because of the teaching or just that the chair was uncomfortable. Once Minister Tomkins was done, the elder Pastor Tomkins then got up to close out the Bible Study.

"I appreciate Minister Tomkins stepping in tonight. Bible Study is good, because it's where we can all come together and learn and gain understanding of the Bible. With that said, I'm going to have to correct my son on part of his message. And since he stood before us all and taught wrong information, then I am going to have to correct him before all. As most of you know, this church was founded by my grandfather. My father succeeded him, and I succeeded my father. When my grandfather founded this church, he founded it on the premise that we are all God's children—every man, woman, and child. That has been the motto of this church ever since. To be honest, I've never personally looked for Scriptures to support it. I never felt that I had to. I do know that there must be at least one verse in the Bible to support it, because my grandfather and my father would not have repeated it if it wasn't. Minister Tompkins, son, I know that you meant well, but this is exactly why I let my ministers teach Bible studies, because it's how you all learn too. We are **all** God's children, and we are always learning regardless of which side of the pulpit we're on."

Susan was confused. As she looked around the room, she could see that she was not the only one. Poor Minister Tomkins. He looked absolutely dejected, and his message was not wrong. What he just taught was truth. It was not a new truth either, as so many these days are teaching, as if God could change. What Minister Tomkins had just taught was the unchanging truth that Jesus spoke of when He said to His once-believing audience in John 8 that "you will know the truth, and the truth shall make you free." Tradition had kept

Susan and many other believers bound for too long in this church, freed but not free. She knew this entire night to be a move of God, in answer to her prayer. Through her pastor's own son, and most likely no longer his successor, God was desiring to shift the paradigm, as well as tear down the strongholds, of tradition.

As her pastor stood before them, blatantly and ignorantly rejecting the truth, Susan quietly prayed, "Our Father in Heaven, what do I do?"

In that moment, she…

FINISH IT!

READ

Bible verses that were referenced in the chapter:

- Isaiah 64:6
- Matthew 25:31-47
- John 3:16-121; 8:31-47
- Ephesians 2:8-9

Bible verses to consider when finishing this story:

- Psalm 1:1-3
- Proverbs 9:9
- Hosea 4:6
- Matthew 5:6; 23:15
- John 1:12-13
- 1 Corinthians 9:19-23; 11:1
- 2 Corinthians 11:4 and Galatians 1:8-9
- 1 John 3:10-11

FINISH IT!

Chapter 9

Just as Much Now as Then

You do understand that if Victor decided to come back today, there would be no need for another wedding ceremony, right? That means that you are still just as married today, although you're legally separated, as you were the moment you both said, "I do," and the pastor pronounced you husband and wife." Jennifer did not want to hear what her best friend was telling her. She knew that Ramona would not be saying it if it was not true though. She and Ramona had been best friends since third grade, and now having also gone to the same college, they were business partners. The two also gave their lives to Christ at the same time.

While attending a youth revival when they were juniors in high school, the two made the decision without discussing it with each other. The fact that they did not discuss it before doing it is key, since the two of them always reasoned with one another before making what was considered "big moves" for two young people. After giving their lives to the Lord, Ramona shared with Jennifer that she, too, was going to do it regardless of whether Jennifer had. She went on to tell her that even though they discussed a lot of things with each other before making a move, or not, that following Jesus was something that she was willing to do with or without Jennifer, or anyone else. Therefore, there was no need for discussion. Jennifer respected that, because it was exactly how she felt too.

Although Ramona was not yet married, she was very wise when it came to marriage. Some people told Jennifer after she married Victor that it would be better if she made new *married* friends. Their reasoning was that Ramona was beautiful and unmarried, and now the two no longer had anything in common. What they did not say was what they were really thinking. That was that they thought Ramona's attractiveness might cause problems for Jennifer and Victor when Jennifer's began to fade. At least one person was bold enough to say what she was thinking, and that was her grandmother. After praying about it, and hearing what God had to say about it, Jennifer decided to remain best friends with Ramona. She was glad that she had. Ramona posed no threat to Jennifer's marriage, and Jennifer posed no threat to Ramona's singleness. So often, married people are given the advice to not have single friends, and sometimes the advisors are right. However, that advice should be on a case-by-case basis.

The two women celebrated each other's marital status. They did so because they knew that just as He gave it to Jennifer to be married and serve Him, that God had also given Ramona the grace to be single and serve Him. Truth be known, unmarried, Ramona could do and go even more for God. Both were learning from each other. Now that Ramona was planning her own wedding, she would soon be able to apply the wisdom and the principles that she had learned just by being a close confidante to Jennifer. And, unfortunately, for the past five months, Jennifer was having to put into practice the lessons learned, now reminders, about singleness from being a close confidante to unmarried Ramona.

Victor, Jennifer's husband of ten years, had come home one day and told her that he no longer wanted to be married. Although he seemed to love the Lord when they met, and seemed to love her when they got married, he told her that he had fallen out of love with them both. He said that he was tired of going through the motions and wanted nothing to do with either of them anymore. He packed his things, moved out, and filed for divorce that week. It was not until a couple of months after he moved out that Jennifer saw for herself the real reason that Victor had decided to end their marriage.

While she and Ramona were out shopping for business supplies one day, they ran into Victor and another woman. Unable to turn and run like he looked like he wanted to do, Victor turned his head and looked the other way as he and the woman walked past Jennifer and Ramona. The woman who was with him obviously had no idea who Jennifer was, because she looked at her and Ramona and smiled innocently at them. Eyes filled with tears, Jennifer managed a smile and even a hello. There was no reason that Jennifer should be angry at the woman; and to her surprise, she felt compassion for her. She learned shortly after Victor left that there had been a number of other women in the past year. One of the women even attended their church. After hearing that Victor had left, the woman went to Jennifer right before a worship service one Sunday morning, and tearfully confessed. She also asked Jennifer to forgive her.

Soon after that, Jennifer learned of at least two other women that her husband had cheated on her with. She had no idea if the woman that he was with now was long-term or a fling. The woman from church and the other two women were apparently only one-night stands. Since she did not plan to ever ask Victor any questions, Jennifer considered what came to her from either the women themselves or from others to be the truth. Not once did she go searching for answers, because to do so would be to bring even more harm to herself. Her prayer to the Father was that if she did not have a need to know that she did not want to know. However, she also knew that the devil was having a field day with this and that he was the main one sending information her way. Regardless to how it came, she decided to view it all as being for her healing. It hurt, but with each bit of news, she stood on Romans 8:28 and declared, "This too is working together for good."

One day, as she was sitting and quietly thinking on the turn that her life had taken, she remembered the time that she had cut her thumb. Victor had warned her to turn the butter knives blade-down when she loaded them in the dishwasher, but she ignored him. She was used to loading them blade-up for years and had not gotten cut. Well, one day she did. In her haste to unload the dishwasher, she cut her thumb on a butter knife. The cut was quite deep, and the bleeding would not stop no matter how much pressure she put on it. So, she did a walk-in visit to her doctor's office. When she was taken in for vitals, one of the first things that the nurse did was remove the bandage from the wound, telling Jennifer, "I'm taking this off because the wound needs to air out." The nurse then began to squeeze the wound. She apologized to Jennifer for making it hurt more, but she also told her that it was necessary for the wound to heal well. That is what it was like with each new report of Victor's alleged indiscretions. *A squeezing.*

Although she knew that *this*, each new discovery was somehow working together for her good, she hoped that the squeezing would stop. The initial pain that came with Victor telling her that he wanted a divorce was more than she could handle. It was like a ripping apart of flesh! When God said that the man and the woman shall become one flesh, that means that they become conjoined at marriage; and the only way to separate them, other than by death, is to rip that flesh apart. Jennifer winced at the thought of that because that is what she was living. Victor had chosen to put them asunder, to rip apart what had become one, making it two again, and she did not understand how he could look so…*unaffected?* "But he was used to acting," she concluded.

"I feel as though my whole marriage was a lie. No, not just my whole marriage, the entire chapter of my life that included Victor. Why didn't he just leave me alone? Instead, he decided to woo me with stories about his experiences with God, and he even had the nerve to go to church with me and to pray with and for me. Thing is, God apparently heard him, because there were many times that he prayed, and God answered."

"But, Jen, you have to stop and think. Think back. Victor was not pretending when you met him. He really did have a relationship with our heavenly Father. He loved the Lord, and it was apparent that he did. Not even the best actor could be that convincing. He also loved you. I don't know when it changed, but he wasn't acting in the beginning." Once again, Ramona was telling Jennifer something that she needed to hear. "One thing that you can't keep doing is blaming yourself. Victor made decisions based on his own desires, not based on anything that you did or did not do. Maybe one day, the two of you you will be able to come together and talk about this, but even if you don't, believe this: You did not drive Victor away. Victor was led away by his own lusts."

"I know that what I'm about to say might be hard for you to hear, but pray for Victor. Don't pray for your marriage to work out. Pray for Victor's soul and his relationship with the Father." Seeing the look on her friend's face, Ramona continued. "If you find that hard to do, then you need to ask yourself if you were pretending too, when you said that you loved him. Yes, he hurt you, but think about Jesus hanging on that cross. He was hurting in every way imaginable, but He rose above all the physical, emotional, and spiritual hurt that we caused Him and hurt for us. He then prayed, "Father, forgive them for they know not what they do." Rise above the hurt that Victor has caused you until you hurt *for* him. Then, like Jesus, pray for him. Even the other women. When you do, you'll discover that somewhere along the way you got your healing."

Tearfully, Jennifer asked her friend, "Will you pray with me?" That was freeing for Jennifer because up until now, all her requests for prayer were, "Will you pray **for** me?" It was only a selfish prayer request though if she kept asking it after being redirected by the Holy Spirit through Ramona to submit this new request. She believed that those prayers for her by Ramona and others whom she had asked to pray for her are what God used to get her to this moment of agreeing to pray for her offenders – Victor and all the other women. She was also convinced that Jesus, above all else, was always living to intercede for her.

"Uh, Jennifer," Alex, one of Ramona's and her business' vendors, said quickly as Jennifer was about to press the red button on her phone.

Hearing him right before pressing the button, Jennifer asked, "Did you say something, Alex?"

"I did. Jennifer, I was wondering if you might want to have dinner with me sometime. I mean, I heard about you and Victor, and I'm sorry to hear that y'all are divorcing; but at the risk of being looked upon as an opportunist, I would like to get to know you outside of work. You know, like personally."

In her mind, she could hear the words that Ramona (no, **GOD**) had spoken to her, *"If Victor came back today and told you that he wanted to get back together, and you agreed, there would be no need for another ceremony. Until the divorce is final, you're just as married today..."* Whispering aloud, Jennifer finished the statement, "'...as when the pastor pronounced us husband and wife.' Yeah, I know, I know." After several months, her divorce was still not final. However, that did not stop Victor from moving on though, and Jennifer could feel the anger for her husband rising once more.

Taken aback, Alex asked, "When the pastor pronounced *who* husband and wife? Jennifer, I'm not asking you to marry me. I would just like to spend some time with you and get to know you outside of work. So, what do you say," he asked.

In that moment, Jennifer...

FINISH IT!

Juanita E. Davis

READ

Bible verses that were referenced in the chapter:

- Matthew 19:6 and Mark 10:9
- Luke 23:34
- Romans 8:28

Bible verses to consider when finishing this story:

- Psalm 1:1-3
- Exodus 20:14
- Proverbs 6:32-33
- Matthew 6:13
- 1 Corinthians 10:13
- Ephesians 4:17-32

FINISH IT!

Meet the Author

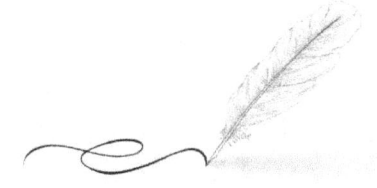

Juanita is a native of Clemson, South Carolina, and a United States Air Force veteran. She met and married Randy, also an Air Force veteran, when they were both stationed at Seymour-Johnson Air Force Base, in Goldsboro, North Carolina. Together they have four grown sons, to whom it was Juanita's pleasure to serve as a stay-at-home mom until their youngest son graduated from high school.

In 1995, while she was still in the military, Juanita heard the call from the Lord for ministry. It came one day when she was nervously preparing to brief other Airmen on preventative medicine. Her Superintendent, who saw her nervousness, told her that God wanted her to know that it was okay that she thought of herself as common. It was okay, because God wanted her to know that He could use that for His glory. Her Superintendent then quoted 1 Corinthians 1:26-29 to her.

Since that day, Juanita has gone on to serve alongside Randy in ministry, to teach Bible studies, to speak at conferences, to be a contributing writer in two book collaborations, and to found *The Unoffended Crusades*. Regardless to what she has accomplished, or will accomplish in life, Juanita readily admits that she needs and will always need the Lord in order to be and to do anything. It is for His joy, praise, and renown that she lives; and she would not want it to be any other way.

After North Carolina, by order of the U.S. military, Juanita and her family went on to live in Okinawa, Japan, from 2002 to 2005. From there, they got military orders to relocate to Las Vegas, Nevada, where Randy retired from the Air Force in 2008. They remained in Las Vegas where they planted *Dominion House Ministries,* in March 2011. In June of 2022, by a direct order from God, the Davises transplanted their household and the church to Randy's hometown of Galesburg, Illinois. One year after the move, Dominion House Ministries merged with another local church, where Randy currently serves as the pastor.

Juanita's first book is titled, <u>A Message for the Disciples...You Too, Peter</u> (2009). It was re-released as <u>You Too, Peter: 15th Anniversary Edition</u>, in December 2024, and can be purchased at most retail outlets where books are sold.

Prayer

God, our Father in Heaven, thank You for the soul that is reading this right now. I ask that You look upon her, and that she would, in turn, look to You for wisdom and for guidance in her every *in that moment*. Your Word says if any lack wisdom, they should ask You, Father, Who gives it generously to all without finding fault, and it will be given to them. Therefore, may she ever walk with Your beloved Son Jesus, Who is Power and Wisdom. Thank You, Father. In Jesus' name. Amen.

www.ingramcontent.com/pod-product-compliance
Lightning Source LLC
Chambersburg PA
CBHW072105050526
44107CB00099B/520